CO NG

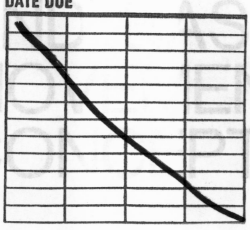

About the authors

Dr. Jane A. Mott, currently a professor and Chairman of the Physical Education Department at Texas Woman's University, earned her doctoral degree at the University of Southern California with an emphasis on research and physiology. Her experience in conditioning and body mechanics has encompassed work with elementary, secondary, and college level students. She has taught at colleges and universities in California, Massachusetts, Nebraska, and Texas, and immediately prior to coming to Texas Woman's University had been the Director of Physical Education at Smith College for sixteen years. Dr. Mott is the author of *Soccer and Speedball for Women* in the William C. Brown Physical Education series and has written for the *Research Quarterly, JOHPER*, and other professional journals and books. She is a former Vice President of the AAHPER and Chairman of the Division for Girls and Women's Sports, a Past President of the Eastern Association for Physical Education of College Women and is presently the Secretary-Treasurer of the American Academy of Physical Education.

CONDITIONING AND BASIC MOVEMENT CONCEPTS

Physical Education Activities Series

Jane A. Mott
Texas Woman's University

SECOND EDITION

Wm C Brown Company Publishers
Dubuque, Iowa

2–07077–02

Contents

Preface

The concept of conditioning developed in these pages is a broad and basic one. Conditioning is not limited to the sole purpose of improved physiological functioning, important as this is. The means taken to normalize the figure, avoid fatigue, reduce tension, solve specific problems amenable to exercise, improve general fitness, and use the body efficiently, effectively, and gracefully, are all encompassed in the author's concept of the term conditioning. Thus, learning to use good body mechanics is one type of conditioning program; weight training for motor fitness and aerobics for physiological fitness are two other types. Conditioning, then, is simply appropriate and prerequisite action to the attainment of specific goals. Through modifications brought about by conditioning it is possible to satisfy very human needs and as a consequence live more fully and richly.

A thorough study of this subject would require several volumes and is clearly beyond the scope of this publication; however, the fundamental concepts, in nontechnical language, are presented here. The key to success is really one of desire. Sustained purpose and practice are necessary in order to replace old habits with better habits. The process requires wanting, knowing, understanding, and doing.

Self-improvement demands purposeful action and personal discipline. Results will not be manifested overnight; it takes time and if the results finally achieved are to be maintained or if still further improvement is to be accomplished, the motivation to persist and the effort to advance must not waver.

The effort, however, is a very gratifying one. The rewards may be increased confidence and poise, improved appearance and pride, a sense of well-being, social efficiency, reduced tension and less fatigue, the normalizing of weight and figure, more efficient and graceful movement, better general fitness. Worth working for?

Discussions on the why-when-how of sound conditioning and efficient body mechanics are included in this book. With a basic understanding of body structure and function, of the biomechanics of human motion, of the principles of diet control, with information about exercise and exercising and knowledge of what exercise can and cannot do, a student need not just memorize calisthenic routines or depend on printed materials or phonograph records. The physically educated woman will be versed in problem solving and will have acquired sufficient knowledge and analytical power to devise or select a conditioning program directed toward the attainment of her personal goals. After that, it is up to her. Understanding, even appreciation, cannot be substituted for action and effort.

Self-evaluation questions, charts, and checklists pertaining to both knowledge and skill are included in these pages. These should give the reader examples of the kinds of understandings that she should be acquiring and the kinds of action she should be taking in order to make progress toward a totally integrated, sound body which will function safely and efficiently, thus providing for its owner more satisfaction and pleasure in living. Responses to the evaluation questions should be thorough and honest, and additional ones should be devised to stimulate learning and progress.

Texas Woman's University students who were subjects for the photographs were Carol Carter, Janelle Krug, and Debra Mitchell. Annette Stender prepared several of the illustrations. The author is most appreciative of the contributions of these people.

A look into the mirror and the future

1

Mobility is a characteristic of all living organisms, and human beings are among the more active and versatile in their movements. Even during sleep or unconsciousness, people roll, turn, twist, snore, and sometimes talk; circulorespiratory and digestive processes continue automatically as do other physiological functions. While awake, it is rare to see anyone in complete repose for more than a few consecutive moments.

Have you ever stopped to realize that bodily movement is the sole means by which we express ourselves, turn our intentions into action, and communicate with the world around us? Speech depends upon muscular control of breath, mouth, and throat; the written word is first produced by hand; even thought processes have their motor components. Characteristic gestures, postures, and facial expressions distinguish individuals one from another. The lift of an eyebrow, a smile, an impatient shrug, or a droop of the shoulders clearly conveys our emotions.

Movement is both a reflection of the inner self and a determinant of the inner self. As you develop the capacity to move effectively and freely, you will feel effective and free. When you acquire the energy needed to perform heavy or prolonged work, you will have banished much of the fatigue and lassitude that plague so many people. If you use exercise as a tool to reshape your body into more aesthetically pleasing proportions your sense of self value will be heightened.

Through physical movement and understanding the concepts related to it, you can change YOU for the better. The process is called conditioning. It encompasses development of basic physical abilities such as strength, flexibility, and endurance. It also includes improvement of motor skills and the acquisition of knowledge about body structure and function. If conditioning accomplishes its purposes, there should be good messages from your body inward to you and outward to others.

Discovery of a compelling reason for a personal conditioning program is a most important step. It is, in effect, a declaration that exercise is going to work for you rather than that you are merely going to work to exercise. As you read through the discussion of "Why Exercise?" select one or more objectives in their order of importance to you.

WHY EXERCISE?

1. What you see in a three-way mirror may provide your incentive to start a conditioning program. Are you satisfied with the reflection? Do certain parts which ought to be firm seem flabby? Do you carry built-in cushions on your hips, thighs, waist, or abdomen? Most figure faults can be improved. If you have failed your mirror test, a more attractive appearance may be your chief concern.
2. Step on the scales. Almost no one exclaims with joy at the poundage registered. True, a few can't seem to gain an ounce, but the majority would gladly share with them. Exercise is essentially a normalizer. If your goal is to gain or lose, an exercise program will be an important adjunct to your diet.
3. Think about the sports, dance, or gymnastic activities you know. Have you experienced the pleasure that comes from performing really well? There are beauty, rhythm, ease, and grace in the movements of the expert. Such harmony is possible only in the body and mind that will do your bidding, that have been trained to be responsive. If you aspire to proficiency, a specific conditioning program tailored to develop the skill, strength, agility, and endurance needed for your purpose may be helpful.
4. The next time you have a chance to "people watch," observe the positions they assume in sitting, standing, and moving about. Regardless of the body's shape or size, it can be held and moved either with grace or awkwardness. It is no small feat to manage skirts that are short, tight, or long and billowy, purses, stoles, high heels, and other accoutrements of feminine attire. Chairs that are deep and low, sports cars, or stairways sometimes shake one's self-assurance. There are ways to conceal as well as to improve figure faults, and there are knacks to accomplishing difficult tasks inconspicuously. Improving your body mechanics may be high on your list of goals.
5. Tension in one form or another is almost inescapable. Noise, crowded conditions, long travel distances, competition, and a host of other factors combine to create physical, mental, and emotional stresses. Have you found yourself twisting your hair, chewing pencils, tapping your feet, lying awake even when dead tired? Tied up in knots before an examination? Stiff and clumsy when you try to hit a ball? How do your neck and shoulders feel after driving an automobile for several hours? Not all of these symptoms arise from the same kind of tensions, but all, to some degree, are under voluntary control. A faithfully pursued program of conscious relaxation can work wonders.
6. Have you a special problem that can be alleviated or corrected by specific exercise? Many troublesome complaints fall into this category. Rehabilitation exercises are essential after certain injuries. Postural faults can

be improved by appropriate exercise when coupled with a real desire for improvement. Dysmenorrhea, aching feet, and back pain may well respond to the exercise approach.

7. Consider the question of general physical fitness. In work and play certain parts of the body are used much more often than others. Many sports, such as the racket games, are one-sided. Bowling and archery demand a keen eye and fine motor coordination but do nothing to improve endurance. Body control is stressed in dance but the manipulation of objects is neglected. You may swim like a fish but have to call for help to open a stuck window. Perhaps you are a fine basketball forward but can't touch your toes with your fingertips. You may huff and puff after you dash up a flight of stairs. There is specificity in the development of strength, flexibility, and endurance just as there is in the acquisition of motor skills. Unless your exercise habits are unusually well-rounded and also very strenuous, you are apt to neglect muscle groups and some elements of overall physical fitness. A general conditioning program can assure you a well-balanced workout.

YOUR PLANS

There is certain information which you need before you can intelligently plan your program. What do you know about the structure and function of the human body, about different kinds of exercise? You can find thousands of calisthenics in books and magazines but which will further your aims? Can you pick the right exercises? Do you know how to adapt them for your purposes? Indeed, do you know what exercise will and won't do? This book was written to give you basic concepts so that you can devise or select an exercise regimen that will meet the changing objectives and needs during the course of your life. The purpose is to help you understand the science of educating your body, learn the art of keeping it in good running order, and experience the joy of moving well.

The physical you,
form and function

2

The physical you includes what you are, how you are put together, and how the body operates in relation to movement and exercise. An understanding of these components of self aids in setting realistic goals for your conditioning program and makes sense of the steps you will need to take to achieve your purposes.

BODY FORM

The human body is a marvelously designed organism, sufficiently nonspecialized to be remarkably adaptable. Its basic size, shape, and proportions are determined by the skeleton, and to that extent an individual's appearance is fixed. We see racial, family, sex, and other group characteristics in skeletal structure. Bone growth and contour can also be affected by such factors as nutrition, disease, and exercise. For practical purposes, however, we must accept our bony structure as it is.

The skeleton provides a study but mobile framework that encloses the vital organs. The framework, in turn, is encased in tissues which produce motion via joint action and serve as a protective cushion for the bones and vital organs. Parts of the skeleton form a system of levers whose actions are powered by muscles generally arranged in pairs crossing one or more joints.

Body type, which is a matter not only of bones but of proportion of musculature and fatty tissue, is also a relatively fixed aspect of appearance. Individuals may be stocky, average, or slender in build. Somatotyping is a system whereby persons can be classified numerically from 1 to 7 according to the degree to which they show characteristics of each body type. A person with a 2-6-3 somatotype evidences the least tendency toward endomorphy or stocky build (2), a little more toward ectomorphy or slender build (3), but is predominately a mesomorph or medium build (6).

Each of us must live within his own body, recognizing its potentials, and accepting its limitations. At high levels of motor performance, as in Olympic competition, it is apparent even to the untrained eye that body form as well as skill influences success. Participants in throwing events tend toward large frame and stocky build, basketball players often are tall and lean, long distance runners frequently are short and lean and women gymnasts more often than not are short and slender but muscular and narrow in the pelvis. Mesomorphy is the component of body build most often noted in athletes in general. Although body build has an influence on motor performance, whether it be sports, dance, or physical labor, many other factors contribute even more. Countless individuals have achieved excellence despite a body type not well-suited to their activity.

Few women aspire to Olympic-level athletic achievement, but many yearn for a sylphlike silhouette. It is best to face facts at the outset. If you have a broad frame and heavy bones and musculature, you cannot become a sylph. There are contours and body proportions pleasing to each body type, however, and these should be your aim. Exercise and diet cannot alter the fundamental body type but they can help a great deal to prevent extremes within a type.

BODY FUNCTION

Discussion of the functional processes of the human body properly includes description of all systems and their interrelationships. It will suffice for our immediate concern with body movement and conditioning to acquire a general understanding of the muscular, circulatory, and respiratory systems.

Muscular System   Physiologists recognize three types of muscle tissue: smooth, such as tissue that functions automatically in the digestive system; cardiac, which is heart tissue; and striated, which is under voluntary control. It is the last type that is your direct concern in conditioning, although indirectly all are affected. The ingenious structure and arrangement of the muscular system permit infinite variety in human motion.

A muscle performs work by actively contracting (shortening) across a joint. The joint acts as a fulcrum, and the bones to which the muscle is attached are brought closer together. In order for this to occur, the muscles on the other side of the joint must lengthen. In general, while one muscle group contracts, the antagonistic muscle group relaxes. Stretching, or lengthening, by relaxation is a passive process, a release of tension rather than a positive action.

Starting in a resting state of slight contraction called *tonus*, a muscle may respond to a stimulus not only by actively contracting to perform work or by passively releasing tension to let itself be lengthened but by contracting to resist being stretched. The synchronization of function between opposing muscle groups is easily understood by considering movement at the elbow. The biceps and triceps muscles do not work independently of other muscles, but the relationship of these two illustrates the action of pairs of muscles.

One end of the biceps is attached to the inner side of the forearm and the other end to the upper side of the scapula (shoulder blade). The muscle thus lies across the elbow joint and acts as a door spring. The triceps, which works in opposition to the biceps, is located somewhat similarly on the back of the arm. As the biceps contracts, the forearm is drawn into closer proximity to the upper arm. The movement normally is facilitated by the simultaneous relaxation of the triceps. On the other hand, when the triceps shortens, the biceps is lengthened and the movement of the arm is reversed, that is, straightened or extended. Should the biceps and triceps exert equal force simultaneously, the elbow is stabilized so that it can neither bend nor straighten from its starting position. When antagonistic muscle groups exert equal force so that no movement occurs, the action is called *static contraction*. *Concentric contraction* is the term applied when a muscle shortens as it contracts. On the other hand, when a contracting muscle is lengthened by an opposing force, the movement is known as *eccentric contraction*.

In considering the work muscles perform, the effect of the force of gravity must be taken into account. Muscles don't have to work when gravity can do the job. In a standing position, the flexor muscles behind the knee must contract actively to kick the lower leg backward. If, instead, the starting position is sitting in a chair with the leg held out in front of the body, gravity will cause the lower leg to fall to a vertical position without assistance from the knee flexors. By contracting the extensors crossing the top of the knee, one can resist the pull of gravity and hold the leg straight as long as the strength of the extensors allows. A slow, controlled knee flexion is obtained if the contracted extensors are gradually relaxed.

Circulatory System   Muscles, like all tissues of the body, require nutrients and oxygen and the elimination of waste products in order to function. The heart and blood vessels serve as the transport system in this process.

The heart is a pump, a muscular organ which by contracting pushes the blood into the arteries. The arteries, tubular vessels, sequentially contract, relax and stretch to move the blood into smaller branches of the system. The actual delivery of food and oxygen in exchange for carbon dioxide and other waste products occurs through the thin walls of the smallest vessels, called "capillaries." Each muscle fiber is in contact with at least one capillary.

At this point, the return of the blood to the heart begins, first through small veins and then, as the veins join, through larger veins. Venous return is mostly an uphill job performed in opposition to the force of gravity. Since veins, unlike arteries, have few muscle fibers, the task of pushing the blood along depends upon the shortening and thickening of striated muscles as they contract and thus exert pressure on the veins. The action of the abdominal muscles is also important in aiding the uphill flow of blood through the very large veins in the abdomen. In addition, veins are supplied with one-way valves to prevent a reversal in the direction of the blood flow.

When the blood reaches the heart it is shunted to the lungs. These are comprised of numerous tiny air sacs, in aggregate resembling a sponge. An exchange of oxygen from the inhaled air and carbon dioxide from the bloodstream takes place through the thin cell walls of the "alveoli," as the air sacs are called. The freshly oxygenated blood is then sent back to reenter the heart. Here, the entire circulatory cycle begins anew.

Respiratory System   The external respiratory system includes the nose, mouth, air passages, lungs, and the muscles which control the breathing process. Air is drawn in from the nostrils or mouth, then passes through the air passages, pharynx, trachea, and bronchial tubes. The bronchial tubes branch successively into smaller air passages terminating in the alveoli. The principal muscles that contract to bring about the inspiratory phase of breathing under resting conditions are the diaphragm and the intercostal muscles between the ribs. Other muscles, particularly the oblique and transverse abdominal muscles, play an important role in increasing the depth of respiration under the demands of exercise.

Why we move and the science of doing it well

$$3$$

Before you read farther, call to mind three motor tasks: exercises, housework chores, sports or dance techniques, or whatever you like. You will find that each task has at least one of the following purposes:

1. To maintain equilibrium.
2. To move something from one place to another.
3. To stop an object in motion.

The first purpose may be the only goal as, for example, when we use our muscles to hold a stationary body position. Movements are very small in this kind of action, but no matter how motionless we try to be, we must continually contract some muscles while others relax in order to resist the pull of gravity and to maintain balance. The maintenance or regaining of equilibrium is always a component in the accomplishment of the second and third purposes of movement. The second purpose is exemplified by such means of locomotion as walking, running, jumping, and crawling, and in moving objects from one place to another as when someone throws, strikes, or lifts them. The third purpose is evident in catching a ball, landing after a jump, or receiving a soccer pass.

Such actions as locomotion, pushing, pulling, throwing, or striking objects (that may come in awkward shapes, sizes, and weights) are involved in both the routine work and the play of normally healthy individuals. The same movements are incorporated in conditioning exercises, games, and dance and are essential in many occupations. Regardless of purpose, all physical actions are governed by biomechanical principles. Movements that are efficient are appropriate to the task and economical of energy. If they are done with a minimum of effort and extraneous motion, the action is satisfying or comfortable to the doer. Usually it is also pleasing to the eye.

When the work load is light, as in picking up a pencil from the floor, the only concerns are accomplishment of the job and appearance. If you remember that you almost always look better with your hips lower than your shoulders, you should get into no trouble by doing what comes naturally. Laws relating to leverage, application of force, and momentum assume importance when the object to be manipulated is heavy. If principles of good biomechanics are violated, awkwardness, fatigue, and injury may result. You will perform everyday tasks, master sports and dance skills, and reach your goals in a conditioning program more easily if you apply the following principles to whatever form of exercise you undertake.

MAINTAINING EQUILIBRIUM

The force of gravity must be constantly resisted to maintain any position other than one in which you are resting entirely supported. Static balance refers to the holding of a fixed body position; dynamic balance is the maintenance of equilibrium while doing something or going somewhere. In either case, maintaining balance is a matter of making the body stable. Two terms are helpful in understanding the concepts involved.

The center of gravity is the balance point of an object, the point about which the weight of the object and the forces affecting it are evenly distributed. The level of the center of gravity of the human body standing upright is about two inches above the hip joint, slightly higher in males than in females. In diving, high jumping, and many other sports or dance techniques, the center of gravity, the point about which the body rotates, is actually located in space outside of the body. The gravity line is an imaginary line, perpendicular to the earth, running through the center of gravity of the body. Thus the line of gravity runs approximately through the center of the upright human body from head to toe. When the center of gravity is shifted laterally, the gravity line is also displaced. Gravitational pull affects all objects within the earth's atmosphere, but the force exerted has most effect on the parts of an object that are farthest from the line of gravity and highest above the center of gravity.

A. A BODY IS IN EQUILIBRIUM WHEN ITS CENTER OF GRAVITY IS OVER ITS BASE OF SUPPORT.

The base of support is the surface on which the body rests. Sometimes there is more than one point of contact with the surface, as in standing on two feet or in assuming a position on the hands and knees. The base includes all of the surface area between the supports in such cases.

Balance is most stable when the line of gravity is directly above the center of the base. Equilibrium becomes more precarious when the boundary of the base is approached by the line of gravity, for a small movement may carry the line over the edge.

To apply the first principle to maintenance of static balance you should:

1. Center your body over your feet or whatever provides the base of support.
2. Fix your eyes on a stationary object to help you to detect lateral body motions and to make adjustive movements to recenter your weight.

1. Place a dot where you estimate the center of gravity to be in this pile of blocks. Then draw the gravity line.
2. Can these blocks stand in this position?
3. Which principle of balance is involved?

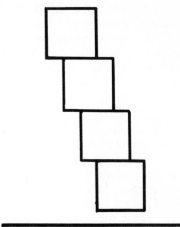

3. Provide friction between the surface and the support. Nonskid footwear, resin on ballet shoes, chalk on the hands, and the selection or treatment of the surface are among the possible means.
4. If standing, grip with the toes to resist changes in position.

B. STABILITY USUALLY IS IMPROVED AS THE BASE IS EN-LARGED.

You might think of the concept this way: as the base of support is enlarged, there is a greater margin of error possible before balance is lost. That is, a wider range of movement must occur to bring the center of gravity outside of the base of support.

There are two ways in which you can apply the principle to maintain static balance:

1. Assume a position in which a larger area of the body makes contact with the base. For example, it is easier to remain poised on the entire foot than to teeter on the ball and toes only.
2. Contact the base with more than one body part. Kneeling, sitting, and all-fours postures involve not only two or more contact points, but incorporate the surface area between the points as part of the supporting base. When standing, the base can be enlarged by separating the feet, but you must use good judgment as to the appropriate direction and degree of separation. In the case of an interfering outside force such as a strong wind or if standing on a tilted surface, the feet should be separated in the direction of the force or tilt. Care must be taken to avoid widening the base so much that the position becomes uncomfortable or that friction between the body and the base becomes insufficient to overcome lateral force. Separating the feet while standing on ice or on skis is an example

of the latter situation. The farther apart the feet, the greater the likelihood that the individual will slide to disaster.

C. STABILITY INCREASES AS THE CENTER OF GRAVITY IS LOWERED.

The potential rotating force of a weight increases as the length of the radius of rotation becomes longer. This radius is the distance from the center of gravity to the center of rotation. If you think of the human body leaning from the ankles, the principle is easily understood. The higher the center of gravity, the fewer are the degrees of tilt required to bring the gravity line outside the boundaries of the base. Thus, the margin of error before equilibrium is lost is decreased. To improve balance, the center of gravity is lowered in order to shorten the radius of rotation.

If tilted to the position shown in the figure, A will fall, but B will rock back to the upright. Which principles of balance are operative?

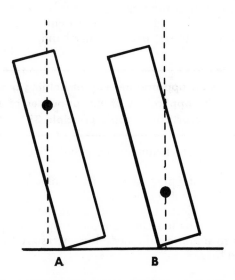

A   B

Again there are two general approaches to applying this principle to holding static positions:

1. When standing, flex the body; in particular, bend the knees and hips to bring the weight center closer to the supporting surface.
2. Assume a position such as kneeling or sitting in order to lower the center of gravity.

D. AN EXTERNAL WEIGHT SUPPORTED BY THE BODY INFLUENCES THE LOCATION OF THE CENTER OF GRAVITY.

For all intents and purposes, an external object that you support becomes a part of your body. The center of gravity and the gravity line are shifted in the direction of the weight. If the object weighs very little, it may be managed in any natural way, but if it is heavy you must adjust your balance and find a means of conserving energy. The guides to maintaining equilibrium given under the first three principles are all applicable but it may be helpful to take special note of the following points:

1. Hold the object close to you, supporting it, if feasible, against the pelvis or thigh. The farther from the center of the base the object is held, the greater will be its effective weight and the resultant disturbance of balance. Muscular fatigue results in changes in body position which disturb balance. Since the arms, shoulders, and back are not so strong as the legs, it is advisable to have a large portion of the weight of the object borne by the legs.
2. Incline the body away from the object by leaning from the ankles keeping the back straight. Such a shift of weight counteracts the force exerted by the object and helps to centralize the line of gravity over the base. The straight back position ensures that the relatively weak back muscles will be minimally involved in the task.
3. Distribute the external weight evenly. For example, you will find it easier to carry two small suitcases, one in either hand, than one large piece of luggage.

Can you demonstrate an appropriate way of holding a heavy sack of groceries and describe the application of the principles of balance, numbers 1, 2, 4, 5? Why is it impractical to apply principle 3?

Again, the purpose is to maintain the gravity line directly over the supporting base.
4. Widen the base by stepping forward if the object is carried in front of the body, or to the side if the object is at the side.
5. If carrying a heavy object in one hand, bend the elbow slightly to relieve strain on the joint. At the same time move the nonsupporting arm away from the body to minimize the body lean necessary to center the line of gravity over the base.

E. A SHIFT ON ONE SEGMENT BEYOND THE BASE MUST BE COMPENSATED FOR BY A SHIFT OF ANOTHER PART OR PARTS IN THE OPPOSITE DIRECTION FOR BALANCE TO BE MAINTAINED.
   Basically, the adjustment that must be made.is a relocation of sufficient body weight to bring the center of gravity back over the base. The principle is violated in the following demonstration and equilibrium cannot be maintained. Standing with your heels against a wall, try to bend forward to touch your toes. It cannot be done, for the wall prevents the hips from moving backward as they would normally do to compensate for the weight shift forward.
   Application of this principle is made, for the most part, without deliberate effort. The sensation of balance disturbed triggers unconscious bodily

adjustments. For example, in walking a narrow balance board, it is instinctive to hold out the arms and use them to make small adjustive movements.

Compare the two positions of the body shown in the figures. Is the base the same size in each? Which is the more stable position and why?

 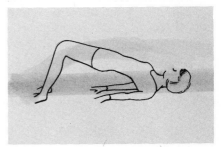

MOVING FROM ONE PLACE TO ANOTHER

If you are the object to be propelled you can walk, run, climb, jump, hop, leap, roll, slide, or fall. The same general mechanical principles apply whether you or something else is to be moved and regardless of the type of work done: pushing, pulling, and so forth. The concepts influencing equilibrium must still be observed but, in addition, you should consider principles governing the application of force and motion.

F. THE FORCE REQUIRED TO MOVE AN OBJECT LINEARLY DECREASES THE MORE NEARLY THROUGH THE CENTER OF GRAVITY THE FORCE IS APPLIED.

If a bat is swung at a softball at a given speed, the ball will travel farther and in a straighter line if contacted at the intersection of the vertical and horizontal midlines of the ball than if the striking point is off center. Conversely, if rotation of the object is desired as in slicing a tennis ball, the ball will rotate more as the contact point is farther from the center of gravity.

G. WHEN TWO FORCES ACT ON AN OBJECT, THE MOVEMENT IS IN THE DIRECTION OF THE RESULTANT OF THE TWO FORCES.

If forces in a vertical and a horizontal direction are applied to an object, the resultant force is along a diagonal line and is less than the sum of the two forces. A single force exerted in a diagonal direction when the desired movement of the object is horizontal or vertical has the same effect as the application of the two forces. Part of the force is dissipated vertically and the remainder is effective in the horizontal direction. An everyday example is the act of raising a window. The desired movement of the window is vertical, but the push on the window is at an angle since you cannot stand directly below.

Part of the force you exert is therefore wasted as it acts in a horizontal direction. The farther you stand from the window, the less effective will be your push.

H. AN OBJECT REMAINS IN A STATE OF REST OR OF UNIFORM MOTION IN A STRAIGHT LINE UNLESS THE OBJECT IS COMPELLED TO CHANGE ITS STATE BY A FORCE.

This description of inertia is a restatement of Newton's First Law of Motion. It tells us that force must be applied to move a resting object. Once in motion, a given direction and speed can be maintained more easily than a change in either can be initiated. A skillful distance swimmer overcomes inertia and accelerates his speed at the start of a race. He then maintains a constant pace until time for the final spurt. A less efficient performer may waste energy by frequent accelerations and decelerations.

I. THE GREATER THE VELOCITY OF A GIVEN MASS, THE MORE FORCE IT EXERTS.

This principle is especially important when propelling objects. If a ball is to be thrown as far as possible, the distance through which the involved body parts move must be great enough to permit rapid speed to be built up. Also, the muscle contractions must occur in sequence and with increasing velocity starting at the foot and ankle and progressing to the fingers. This progressive action adds the force of each sequential contraction to the next so that the final force is the sum of all.

J. EVERY ACTION CAUSES AN EQUAL AND OPPOSITE REACTION.

This is the meaning of Newton's Third Law of Motion. Expressed more specifically, the forces exerted by two objects in contact are equal in amount and opposite in direction. The reactive force is readily apparent in the rebound of a ball thrown to a wall or in the motion of water toward the feet as a swimmer strokes. The reactive force is useful in these examples, but when a ball is received, the reactive force not only is valueless but may cause discomfort or injury. The task, then, is to receive and react to the force over time and space. This is done by a withdrawing movement of the receiving surface as contact with the object is made. The principle is applied in catching a ball, for example, by giving with the hands and arms, and with the knees and hips too if the throw were hard. The effect is to lessen the initial impact.

GUIDELINES FOR MOVING YOURSELF AND EXTERNAL OBJECTS

The preceding principles governing motion and the application of force do not comprise an all inclusive list. Nevertheless, in conjunction with principles relating to maintenance of equilibrium, they supply most of the rationale for techniques used to move yourself or external objects efficiently and effectively.

Lifting and Lowering

1. Get close to the object; lift or lower as vertically as possible.
2. Use both hands if the object is very heavy.
3. Bend the knees and keep the back relatively upright, for its muscles are not designed for heavy lifting.

Fig. 1   Lifting—the wrong way   Fig. 2   Lifting—the right way

Pushing

1. Enlarge the body surface that contacts the object. For example, use the shoulder as well as the hands.
2. Apply force at two points equidistant from the center of gravity if direction of the push is difficult to control.
3. Apply force at a point away from center of gravity if object is to be moved in a rotatory direction.
4. With the feet back from the object, angle body toward it from the ankles.

Fig. 3   Shoving—the wrong way   Fig. 4   Shoving—the right way

Pulling

1. Use both hands if the object is heavy; stabilize the arm position before pulling.
2. With feet near the object, angle the body away from it from the ankles.
3. Pull in an upward as well as a forward direction if there is much friction between the object and the supporting surface.
4. Use a tow rope fastened no higher than the center of gravity if the object is weighty and large.

Throwing and Striking

1. Apply force through the center of gravity of the object if a straight path of projection is desired, or off center if rotatory motion is the purpose.
2. For accuracy, keep the point of release or contact consistent, and line up the throwing arm or striking implement with the target.
3. For distance:
   a. Separate feet in the direction of the intended line of projection.
   b. Lengthen the backswing.
   c. Involve the entire body in the back and forward action by rotating, bending, and straightening.
   d. Apply force in sequence from the supporting foot through the joints involved to point of impact or release.
   e. Use a preliminary step, run, or hop and then transfer weight in the direction of the hit or throw.
   f. Speed up the preparatory and propulsive movements.
   g. *Follow-through*, avoid slowing down or changing direction at the point of release or impact.
   h. Select the angle of release or contact that is appropriate for the object and the force applied to it. A projection angle of roughly 45 degrees gives maximum distance in throwing.

Walking and Running   These two forms of locomotion are so vital to almost every aspect of daily living that they are discussed at length in Chapter 11.

Jumping, Leaping, and Hopping   These activities, like throwing and striking, are projection movements and, like most forms of locomotion, require body balance to be lost and then regained on landing. Rather than keeping a stable body position with the center of gravity centered over the base, the body weight must be shifted off center so that movement can occur. For greatest distance do the following:

1. Incline body in the direction of the intended movement.
2. Flex ankles, knees, and hips preliminary to takeoff.
3. Rock to balls of feet and swing arms back and forth several times prior to takeoff.
4. Use a very large arm swing timed to give impetus to the takeoff.

5. Take off from the balls and toes of the feet.
6. Continue the body motion in same line of direction after landing.

STOPPING AN OBJECT IN MOTION

Stopping moving objects is basic to many sports, dance, and exercise movements. Almost every kind of ball game involves catching, blocking, trapping, or otherwise receiving an impetus. The body itself must be stopped after a run, leap, or gymnastic movement. The difference between the two situations is that in the first the body or an implement it holds is the receiving surface and must adjust to the force that is met. In the second instance, the body is the force and must adjust to meet a surface.

Catching or Blocking

1. Assume a position, stationary if possible, in line with the oncoming object.
2. Take a stride stance toward the object.
3. Lower the center of gravity by bending at the hips, knees, and ankles.
4. "Give" as the object touches the body.
5. Keep your eyes on the object.
6. Wear a glove or mitt for catching when possible.
7. If catching, reach toward the object and on contact pull it in to the body.
8. Point the fingers up for catching objects above the waist, or down for objects below the waist, but never at the object.
9. If blocking a moving object with the head or abdomen, as in soccer, move forward to meet the object and tense the muscles receiving the stress.

Landing

1. Land first on the balls of feet, except in broad jumping, and if momentum is great, take several small running steps, jumps, or a forward roll.
2. "Give" at the hip, knee, and ankle joints.
3. If jumping from a height, first lower the center of gravity to diminish the landing force.
4. If jumping from a moving object, land in a forward stride position and run in the direction the object is going.
5. Hold the arms out to adjust balance on landing.
6. If about to fall, lean away from the direction of the fall to shift the center of gravity and thus counteract some momentum.

About exercising and exercises

4

"A rose is a rose is a rose," but exercise is not exercise is not exercise. There are different types of exercises, each yielding a different form of dividend. You must match the type to your conditioning goals if you are to gain the rewards you expect.

A variety of programs of exercise is also found. Weight training, Aerobics, Isometrics and Isotonics, Calisthenics, Circuit Training and Interval Training are among the titles currently popular. These are not mutually exclusive, for some of the same results may be had from the different approaches.

TYPES OF EXERCISES

Like games and sports, exercises may be classified by innumerable systems. There are exercises for specific body parts (hips, feet, thighs, etc.); for age groups (teenagers, the middle aged); for occupations (businessmen, housewives); for posture correction (forward head, hollow back); for degree of exertion required (mild, moderate); for health problems (dysmenorrhea, backache). The possibilities are endless, but one of the most useful systems classifies exercises according to their intended effects on the body. Thus we find exercises designed to strengthen, to develop circulorespiratory endurance, to improve flexibility, to relax. These categories are not mutually exclusive but that is unimportant; few exercises are pure in function. One of these purposes is, however, emphasized in most exercises.

Even without precise mechanical analysis, exercises can be judged and sorted with reasonable accuracy. The following should help you determine whether a given exercise can contribute to the purpose you have in mind.

Strengthening Exercises

Strength is one of the most essential attributes to be gained through physical exercise, for a lack of this quality limits the development of skill, flexibility, and endurance. Contrary to popular belief, people do not have to lose flexibility and become "muscle bound" as they gain strength (24).

Strengthening exercises are characterized by forceful muscular contractions. There always is a resistance to be met or overcome. Body weight or external objects may be moved or held in opposition to the force of gravity. Sometimes one set of muscles contracts against a resistance that cannot be moved.

Differences among three types of strengthening exercises should be noted. In *isotonic* exercise overt movement results. The force exerted is sufficient to overcome the resistance provided. Running, arm swinging, bending, jumping, and weight lifting are a few examples. The term "Isokinetic Exercise" refers to a form of isotonic weight training in which speed of movement is mechanically controlled in order to permit maximum muscular effort throughout the entire range of motion. Muscle groups differ in their strength at different angles of the joints involved. The heaviest weight that can be lifted through an entire range of motion is the weight that can be lifted at the angle where the muscle group is weakest. The muscle group, therefore, does not work to capacity at other angles under the usual weight lifting program. *Isometric* exercise illustrates the effect of an irresistible force meeting an immovable object. Effort is exerted, but no observable motion ensues. One set of muscles, for example, may be contracted while an equal opposing action may be provided by the antagonistic muscles. Sometimes the resistance is supplied by a stationary object as in pushing against a wall. Another form of isometric exercise calls for holding an external weight motionless. The muscles to be strengthened are held in a state of contraction for a given length of time.

The role of the force of gravity has to be considered when you wish to develop strength, for you must choose movements in which gravity and the opposing muscles are not doing the work you want a particular muscle group to perform.

How much resistance and how many executions of an exercise will result in the greatest strength gain are questions that have intrigued numerous researchers. Findings indicate that a smaller number of executions against a greater resistance is more effective than vice versa. You will find specific recommendations in the discussion of weight training, Chapter 8.

Stretching Exercises

It is generally accepted that flexibility is an important component of motor fitness. The optimum level of flexibility differs from activity to activity, and an individual's range and ease of mobility are specific to the various joints of the body (16). More than normal flexibility may or may not be advantageous depending on the demands of the specific activity and whether an individual has sufficient strength to control the range of motion.

Stretching or flexibility exercises carry body parts beyond their usual range of motion. Nothing is accomplished by moving only so far as is easy; you must feel some pull to know that muscles are being stretched. Flexibility exercises are slow, sustained, held stretches, or are rhythmically performed and free-swinging actions. There must be periodic increases in the distance the movements cover. The objectives in exercising for suppleness are to lengthen the range without overdoing the action to the point of uncomfortable muscle soreness and to improve the ease with which the motion through the range is made.

Myotatic Reflex   The myotatic, or stretch reflex causes a suddenly stretched muscle to contract in reaction. It is better for this reason to use slow, sustained motions and to hold positions of stretch rather than to bounce, bob, or fling the body into stretch positions from which it may rebound. When the stretch reflex is activated, the sharp contraction which follows seems to increase the possibility of muscle soreness.

Muscular Endurance Exercises

Endurance describes the ability to keep going. Muscular endurance refers to that ability in a muscle or group of muscles. Local fatigue causes the performer to cease the action involved. Muscular endurance requires and is developed by extending the duration of an activity; that is, by increasing the number of executions or the time a position is held. Doing more sit-ups today than yesterday or holding a chin position on the bar longer are exercises which can improve the endurance of the muscles involved.

It has been substantiated that muscular strength and muscular endurance form a continuum with a single maximum effort (strength) representing the near end and a maximum number of executions involving a constant resistance (endurance) representing the far end. The relative proportions of strength and muscular endurance change inversely with the endurance factor being greater at the far end (23) (36).

Exercises for improving muscular endurance may be isotonic or isometric but in either case will emphasize the ability of a muscle or muscle group to continue to perform a given task over a period of time.

Circulorespiratory Endurance Exercises

Circulorespiratory endurance, in contrast to muscular (local) endurance, refers to the ability of the large muscle groups of the body to prolong such generally demanding tasks as running, chopping wood, climbing stairs, or taking part in vigorous sports and dance activities. All life processes, and strenuous exercise even more so, require energy which is produced by the burning of food by oxygen. The more oxygen that can be taken in and utilized for the production of energy, the greater is the circulorespiratory endurance.

As the name implies, this type of endurance is mainly dependent upon the condition of the circulatory and respiratory systems. Maximal oxygen utilization results from much increased heart rate, maximum stroke volume per beat, and maximum extraction of oxygen from the blood (29). Improvement of circulorespiratory endurance is the most valuable benefit of exercise for it enhances the quality of life and may well reduce the incidence or severity of cardiovascular and related diseases (14). This kind of endurance and the term "physical fitness" are synonymous.

The heart muscle becomes stronger and more efficient under conditions of regular exercise of sufficient intensity and duration. In comparison with untrained individuals, persons with a high level of circulorespiratory endurance exhibit larger stroke volumes and lower resting heart rates as well as beneficial differences in oxygen transport (29) (11). In short, they can prolong a given amount of work with less effort and they have a greater work capacity over a period of time.

Exercises for the improvement of circulorespiratory endurance include many sports and dance forms such as basketball, long distance swimming, track events, square dance, and field hockey. Respiration and heart rate speed up in response to the physiological demands. It probably is necessary for the body to warm up enough under normal ambient temperatures to produce sweating for there to be an endurance conditioning effect (10:241-242). Probably it also is necessary for the heart rate to be elevated to approximately 60 percent of its resting to maximum rate range (20:199). For example, with a resting rate of 72 and a maximum rate of 185, the estimated required rate is $72 + (.60 \times 113) = 140$ beats per minute. Finally, research evidence and expert opinion suggest that optimal training effects are obtained from several workouts per week for a minimum of twenty to thirty minutes duration (27). The exercise may alternate between three five-minute bouts of strenuous but not maximal intensity and light activity, or the exercise may be steadier and lower in intensity. (2)

Relaxation Exercises

A muscle is said to relax when contraction of its fibers is lessened. Muscular relaxation is a *letting go*, a release of tension, a reduction, or even complete cessation of movement. Strictly speaking, exercise is the antithesis of relaxation, and yet because certain types of movement are useful in bringing about relaxation, we refer to such actions as relaxation exercises.

Exercises intended to induce relaxation may involve strong muscular contractions. The movements tend to be slow; the effort often is sustained for several seconds; and completion of the action may be an abrupt cessation of the muscular contraction. Frequently, relaxation exercises are performed first with one and then with another part until the entire body has been involved.

General relaxation also is promoted by reducing the heart rate. Most muscular activity increases its pace, but certain movements or body positions which improve the return of blood to the heart permit that organ to decelerate. The venous flow of blood to the heart is mostly against gravity when an individual sits or stands. Circulation from all levels below the heart must overcome the force of gravity. On the contrary, blood returns not only unimpeded but assisted by gravity in exercise which elevates most of the body higher than the heart. If the movement is slow and not very strenuous and particularly if it causes the hips to be held higher than the chest, the heart rate will decelerate. Such deceleration is conducive to general relaxation.

THE OVERLOAD PRINCIPLE

Improvement in strength, flexibility, muscular, and circulorespiratory forms of endurance comes about only through application of the Overload Principle. That is, the task which is performed by the system involved must be greater than the work to which the system is accustomed. You must, for example, push yourself to run farther, jump more times, lift a heavier weight, or move more quickly than is easy. Furthermore, you must continue to increase the task periodically in order for gains in conditioning to continue.

SECOND WIND AND STITCH IN THE SIDE

You may have experienced a phenomenon called second wind. Perhaps while playing some game such as soccer you ran until you thought you would drop. All of a sudden the unpleasant symptoms eased; your breathing quieted down and you were able to forget your fatigue for a while longer. When energy requirements suddenly increase, metabolic adjustments are made. If you push on despite distress signals, a balance will be achieved (10:159). People in an excellent state of training may make the transition to second wind so easily that they are not aware of reaching it. The state of second wind usually is achieved only under the high motivation of competition or with determined perseverance. Some individuals simply never have given that extra measure of effort that leads to the sudden, exhilarating satisfaction of feeling the body shift into high gear and begin to function harmoniously with seemingly unlimited reserves of energy at its command. Of course, even the marathon runner must stop eventually. If exercise is continued, physiological balance gradually will be lost and the body will signal that it has had enough for the time being.

A stitch in the side is nothing to worry about. This familiar pain also seems to be related to adjustments to heavy exercise demands.

TYPES OF EXERCISE PROGRAMS

Isotonic and Isometric Calisthenic Programs

The most universally adaptable of the several types of exercise programs are isotonic and isometric calisthenics. The exercises can be performed without equipment, resistance is supplied by the force of gravity and the individual's own body, space requirements are minimal (you can even exercise in bed), and the exercises can be geared to all ages and various states of health. You can exercise alone or enjoy the company of a group and you can fit the program into your daily schedule wherever you like.

Grasp each end of a bath towel. Now see if you can devise three isometric exercises, one each for strengthening arms and shoulders, neck, and ankles.

Isometric exercise has been widely hailed as the magic producer of fitness. Claims have been made and substantiated for strength gain from a regime comprising as little as one maximum contraction per day. Because people would like to think that "instant exercise" can yield adequate results with little effort, newsstands and bookstores have blossomed with routines of isometric exercise. Now that the furor is subsiding, it is only too apparent that, as with most cherished prizes, the rewards of exercise go to those who work for them. Isometric exercise is good; it can improve strength and muscle tone; the time and equipment demands are modest. It does not, however, supplant isotonic exercise because it contributes negligibly to improvement in circulorespiratory endurance, or to flexibility, or to the development of efficient patterns of movement. Even the strength gained is limited chiefly to the specific angles at which the joints are held during the exercise (10:370-371). A sound general conditioning program, therefore, includes both isotonic and isometric exercise but mostly isotonic (21).

Interval Training Programs

Interval training is a plan whereby short periods of exercise are alternated with short rest intervals. Such a schedule makes good sense, especially when one is concerned primarily with increasing the quantity of work done. Under interval training conditions, a given work load can be managed with less fatigue. Put another way, a work load costing a given amount of energy per minute can be carried on intermittently over a much longer time than if done continuously.

The interval training principle can be applied to any of the purposes of exercise. Alternate work and rest periods of 30 seconds to 5 minutes duration have been found effective. The longer work intervals are more productive when training for endurance (aerobic) events; shorter intervals of greater intensity contribute more to short-term (anaerobic) exertions such as sprints and weight lifting (10:401).

Weight Training Programs

With the veritable mushrooming of opportunities for high level athletic competition, girls and women have turned enthusiastically to weight training as a means of improving performance. This form of exercise is without question the most effective way of developing muscular strength and muscular endurance. Exercises performed in weight training programs may be isotonic, isometric, or isokinetic, provided the apparatus for the last is available. By the use of barbells and weight plates and dumbbells of various sizes, and by adjusting the mechanisms of the numerous types of training machines, it is possible to regulate the work load precisely to suit the capabilities of each individual.

Some of the equipment customarily employed in weight training can be improvised or is light enough in weight and sufficiently inexpensive for home use. On the other hand, much of the apparatus is bulky, costly, and accommodates only one user at a time. The latter conditions are disadvantages of the weight training type of program as is the fact that benefits in circulorespiratory endurance are not easily achieved by this means.

A variable resistance piece of apparatus provided with multiple stations has come into wide use recently. It enables more than one person to engage in different types of exercise simultaneously within a relatively small space. This apparatus, manufactured by several companies, comes in different sizes and offers choices of types of exercise devices.

Circuit Training Program

Circuit training is a plan for accomplishing purposes of exercise by performing a series of tasks numbered in sequence and arranged in a circuit. The participant executes the task at a station a prescribed number of times and then moves to the next station, usually continuing until three circuits have been completed.

The tasks can be any form of exercise appropriate to the conditioning goals and possible in the space available. As proficiency develops, repetitions, resistance or speed of performance may be increased or the task may be changed.

The chief advantages of circuit training are its versatility in types of exercise possible and the tangible evidence of progress.

Aerobics Program

Aerobics, the immensely popular approach to improving physical fitness, was devised and first published by Dr. K. H. Cooper for United States Air Force personnel in 1968 (7). Since then, the growth of interest in the program has been phenomenal.

When sufficient oxygen can be supplied for a task, the work is called "aerobic." The ability to keep going in such tasks depends upon circulorespiratory endurance, or physical fitness, and improvement in this direction is the aim of aerobics. The system is based on the rate of oxygen consumption demanded by various physical activities performed at different intensities. Whether there is much contribution to exercise objectives other than circulorespiratory fitness is determined by the type of activity chosen by the participant. Points are assigned in the aerobics system by which the amount of exercise, no matter what kind, can be judged quantitatively according to the degree of energy expended. Points are accumulated whenever the individual exercises, and a running record of points per week is maintained. A variety of specific exercise programs is offered by age and sex. Standards for development and maintenance of fitness are provided. Further information about conditioning under the aerobics system appears in Chapter 8.

Evaluating and adapting exercises

5

Do you know what a given exercise can do for you? How can you judge whether exercises can or cannot achieve the ends claimed for them? Is it possible to adjust or adapt exercises to make them suitable?

EVALUATING EXERCISE

Every library houses books describing exercises for a multiplicity of purposes. Most textbooks of exercises have been written by physical educators or physicians who are well versed in the anatomy of the human body, in kinesiology, and in activity physiology. A very different situation is encountered in newspapers, magazines, and popular books. Here the qualifications for authorship differ widely.

Health and beauty columns abound with exercise programs for weary office workers, housewives with bulges in the wrong places, husbands with spare tires, and children who spend too many hours glued to the television set. Actually, such exercise series can be good fun and good for you. Trying out a new "daily dozen" is enjoyable, and there is no doubt that the photographs of the models evoke the desire to emulate. Often there are good tips on ways to use household furniture as exercise apparatus. But, *the reader is warned to be wary.* No exercise prescribed by an author with unknown credentials should be accepted on faith. Instead, you should subject the exercises to critical scrutiny.

Ask These Questions   Evaluation of an exercise is not difficult if you ask these questions and answer them correctly.

1. What is the principal action in the exercise?
2. Which body parts are brought closer together?

3. What is the location of the main muscle groups that are shortening, on the front, back, side?
4. Is the force of gravity or muscular contraction primarily responsible for the movement?
5. If the force of gravity brings the body parts closer together are the opposing muscles contracting to resist this force?
6. Which body parts are brought farther away from each other? Is the range of movement larger than can be accomplished with ease?
7. Where is the action felt?

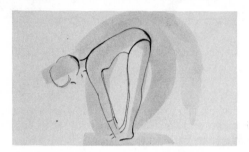

Fig. 5   Toe Touch

For illustrative purposes, consider the toe touching exercise frequently encountered in popular magazines. Usually this is described as a waist trimmer, an exercise to reduce the "tummy." As you think about the exercise and try it out, you will answer the preceding questions by going through a reasoning process somewhat as follows.

The principal action is the movement of the trunk which is brought forward and down toward the legs. The muscle groups that shorten are on the front of the trunk and thighs. The force of gravity produces the action. If

---

Analyze this side bending exercise by asking yourself the seven questions suggested on pages 25-26. What is the main purpose of the exercise?

the reach down toward the toes is done rather slowly, the muscles opposing gravity, which are on the back of the trunk and thighs, will contract to slow down the movement. The trunk and back of the legs are angled away from each other on the downward reach. The range of movement is not easy for most people. The action is felt in the backs of the legs.

On the return to standing position, there is a reversal of the body parts brought closer together and farther apart. Muscular action is essential to lift the trunk in opposition to the pull of gravity. The muscles on the back of the trunk and thighs must contract to produce this action. The movement back to erect standing is well within the customary range of motion. The action is felt in the back muscles.

This analysis seems long and involved in print, but it can be done mentally with only a few moments of thought. You will conclude that the muscular contractions both on the down and up phases of the exercise were performed by dorsal muscles; therefore, the exercise could not by any stretch of the imagination flatten or reduce the tummy. Since the work load of lifting the trunk is relatively easy, it is doubtful that even the back muscles will be strengthened much, although whatever strengthening effect there is will certainly be in that location. Obviously, the action does not quicken the pulse and so this must not be classified as an endurance exercise. Nor are the characteristics of a relaxation exercise present. Of the remaining possibilities, strengthening and stretching, it seems that stretching is the more important. It may be concluded that the development of flexibility in the hamstrings (muscles on backs of thighs) is the main purpose of toe touching.

Cautions   The evaluation of an exercise includes one more step, consideration of safety. If the body is without structural defects and in good physical condition, there is little reason to avoid almost any movement which is structurally possible. All muscles are designed to be used; there is no muscle group that cannot be benefited by exercise. Nor is there reason to cease a strenuous activity until it seems impossible to continue, for there are built-in fatigue signals that induce an individual to stop before he approaches his physiological limit. Nevertheless, people do occasionally harm themselves by exercise, hence a few words of caution.

1. If there is any possibility of circulorespiratory medical problems, violent exercise that demands heavy-weight bearing or that causes much rise in the heart rate may be harmful. A thorough medical examination is the best insurance against this danger or against ill-effects when exercise is contraindicated for any other health reason.
2. A minor ill-effect is muscular soreness. This is uncomfortable but not at all serious and is relieved by heat and by moderate participation in the very movements that brought about the soreness. Flexibility exercises, even more than other types, tend to cause muscular soreness so it is well to increase the number of repetitions and the range of motion gradually and to perform the movements slowly.
3. The leg muscles are very strong, whereas the back muscles are relatively weak. All heavy lifting should be done by stabilizing the back in an erect position and making the legs provide the necessary power.

4. The lower back is a frequently injured area of the anatomy. Not only should you avoid lifting with the back muscles, but you should refrain from sudden, sharp, and very forceful flexion in the lumbar region. An example of a POOR EXERCISE WHICH MIGHT INJURE THE LOWER BACK is as follows: Stand, arms forward at shoulder level, elbows straight and palms on the wall. Flex the elbows and forcefully arch the back to bring the abdomen forward toward the wall.
5. The knee is a hinge-type joint incapable of lateral movement and thus subject to strain if the body weight or an external force exerts sideward pressure. Also, many authorities consider it unwise to perform exercises that require the assumption of a deep knee-bend position.

CHANGING THE DIFFICULTY OF AN EXERCISE

Exercises differ in the physical demands placed on the performer. The qualities of strength, flexibility, agility, and the like are required to a greater or lesser degree as is the expenditure of energy.

When you select an exercise, you may discover immediately that it is unsuitable: either you are not able to do it successfully or you are able to perform it much too easily. In either case, the demands are inappropriate. Even those exercises which seem right initially are likely to challenge you less and less as time goes on. Gratifying as this latter situation may be, it is also a warning that your progress is reaching a stalemate. More taxing effort is plainly indicated.

Principles Involved   An exercise which fails the suitability test because of its level of difficulty need not be discarded. With ingenuity you can alter many exercises via the overload principle. The demands of an exercise can be heightened by increasing one or more of these factors:

1. Speed of the movement.
2. Number of repetitions or time a position is held.
3. Range of the movement or distance over which the body travels.
4. The resistance to be overcome.

The first two factors are self-explanatory, and examples should clarify numbers three and four.

An exercise may be described as touching the fingers to the ankles. You can increase the range of this movement by touching the floor instead or, even more, by placing the palms flat on the floor. The most usual examples of increasing the distance over which the body travels are to walk or run farther than before.

There are alternative applications of the fourth principle. You may increase the resistance to be overcome by using objects such as Indian clubs, dumbbells or weights of any sort. You may change the direction of movement so that the force of gravity has a greater effect. For example, in a push-up from the floor, gravity offers more resistance to the action than it does in a push-up from a lean against the wall. A third possibility for adaptation is to lengthen the lever arm that is to be moved. This happens when a sit-up is performed full length rather than from the knees. Still another alternative is to move body parts so as to make the distribution of weight less well-balanced. The effect of such an increase in the resistance may be convincingly demonstrated: The relatively easy sit-up from a hook-lying position becomes well-nigh impossible if the legs are drawn up until the heels touch the body.

A progression in the difficulty of an exercise might start, for example, with a sit-up from hook-lying position with fingertips touching on top of head. An entire series of modifications can easily be planned to upgrade or downgrade the physical demand. The following list illustrates the application of the principles just discussed:

Can you think of three adaptations of a knee push-up exercise, as described on page 75, in which you change the resistance to be overcome?

SIT-UP SERIES

1. Back-lying position. Lift head and neck, hold five counts, then lower.
2. Hook-lying position. Flatten lower back, lift head and curl up to a 45-degree angle with the floor. Reverse action to starting position.
3. Hook-lying position, arms crossed on chest. Lift head, flatten lower back and curl up to touch elbow to outside of opposite knee. Reverse action to starting position. Repeat.
4. Same as 3, but with fingertips touching top of head.
5. Back-lying position, arms overhead, elbows straight. Jackknife to touch fingers to ankles, hold five counts, then return to starting position. Keep head and back in straight alignment and knees extended throughout. This last exercise should not be attempted until good pelvic control is attained so that the lower back does not arch when the movement is initiated.

Your conditioning program

6

You are now ready to consider your own conditioning program. If your primary goal is improvement of motor or circulorespiratory fitness, exercise is the real key to success. But remember that just any exercise won't do. Differences in type, intensity, speed, and duration bring about very different results. If your conditioning is aimed toward weight control and figure improvement, exercise still is very important but should be combined with diet regulation. The conditioning process for improving body mechanics requires a third approach. Here there is less emphasis on exercise, per se. You must concentrate, instead, on acquiring knowledge of how to do something and then must practice the skill faithfully until it becomes habitual.

PROCEDURES COMMON TO ALL PLANS

1. Set a clear, definite long-term and, if possible, short-term goal (e.g., weight to be lost, distance to be run, technique to be improved, body measurement to be attained). Drastic changes don't occur overnight; be realistic.
2. Determine and record your present status as accurately as possible so that improvement can be measured.
3. Take stock of the forms and amounts of exercise in which you daily engage. Count not only planned but incidental exercise (walking to classes; housework; stair climbing; occupational tasks of lifting, carrying and moving heavy objects). Note activities that contribute to your conditioning purposes. Check also muscle groups or types of exercise that are customarily neglected.
4. Decide which general forms of activities will help you: strength developing calisthenics, dance, sport, jogging, or diet? Then write down the specific activities you intend to do. You may start with a program

outlined in this book or you may adopt "as is" or with modifications a program you have read elsewhere. Even better, make up your own.

5. Prepare a chart or other appropriate record form on which you can keep track of what you do in your program from day to day. Include also a record of changes in your status; for example, strength, distance run in a given time, body measurements and weight, or improvement in body mechanics.

6. Commit yourself to definite days and periods of time for conditioning activities and make note in your appointment book. Don't cheat. Regularity is important. Even three fifteeen-minute sessions a week are adequate for some purposes; for others many hours and daily effort are essential.

7. Find someone to exercise or practice with you if possible. Make a commitment to this person and be on hand at the appointed time.

8. Start each exercise session with warm-ups that get you in the mood and prepare the body for more intense work. Loosen up muscles slowly to avoid injury.

9. Include a workout for the several regions of the body. Use good form; don't give in to lazy, half-hearted efforts.

10. Taper off to close each exercise period.

11. Step up exercise demands by increasing duration, rapidity, frequency, or work load.

12. When you reach your first goal, set another or shift to a maintenance schedule. More effort is needed to build up to a level than to hold it. Trial and error will show you how far you can go without slipping back.

13. Periodically review information you have read in this book. You will want to overlearn the basic principles so that you can readily apply them in the future.

14. Watch for current periodical literature and books which will add to your understandings and keep your information in line with the latest research.

Information to help you accomplish your specific purposes will be found in the remaining chapters. A sample plan for weight control and figure improvement in Chapter 7, pages 37-38 is presented as an example of how to draw up your own program for any conditioning purpose. Descriptions of calisthenic and weight training exercises are given in Appendix A. In addition to reviewing the information in these two sections of the book, you will want to consult Chapter 8 for guides to planning a conditioning program for general fitness through weight training, aerobics, the use of sports and dance, or calisthenics. Chapter 9 has to do with conditioning for participation in sports and dance. Chapters 10, 11, and 12 pertain to conditioning for good body mechanics.

Conditioning for weight control and figure improvement

7

No one wants to look fat or bulgy or risk the physical disabilities with which overweight is associated. An underweight condition more often than not is normal and healthy; obesity, on the other hand, is potentially harmful.

During recent years, Americans have become weight conscious and aware of the difficulties of maintaining normal poundage in a society that fosters sedentary habits. Almost every grocery or drugstore displays dietetic products, and most women's magazines feature articles on weight control. New diets, exercise programs, and mechanical devices purported to slenderize or reshape the body appear with regularity.

Probably as much misinformation as information is circulated about weight control. And perhaps because they want it to work, otherwise rational people with good critical judgment adopt the latest fad in an attempt to solve their weight problems. The unembellished facts of weight control are simple; it is the acquisition of satisfactory habits that is difficult.

Body weight is maintained when there is a balance between intake of food and output of energy. If the equilibrium is upset, the scales reflect the direction of the change. Losing or gaining weight is, therefore, easy in principle. One can eat more or fewer calories and/or exercise more or less.

WEIGHT STANDARDS

The proportions, shape and firmness of the body, not its weight, determine the attractiveness of the figure. Muscles are heavier than fatty tissue, and if you have well-developed, strong muscles you will weigh more but look more slender than someone whose body is soft and flabby. The mirror, the fit of your clothing, and the way you feel are better standards for weight than weight charts but an *estimate* of desirable weight can be made by consulting the weight chart in Appendix B, page 87.

PROPORTIONS AND WEIGHT

(This chart is only a rough guide to proportions. Check with your mirror.)

	Your Present Measurement*	Your Measurement Goal	
Height (barefooted)		x x x x x x x x x x	x x x x
Weight		x x x x x x x x x x	
Wrist		x x x x x x x x x x	x x x x
Bust		x x x x x x x x x x	x x x x
Waist		8-10" less than bust	
Abdomen		1½-2½" less than bust	
Hips		1-3" more than bust	
Ankle		2½" more than wrist	
Thigh		10-13" more than ankle	
Calf		4-5" more than ankle	

*Measure at largest girth, except waist, wrist and ankle which should be measured at smallest part.

After attaining full growth and maturity, at about age twenty-five, body weight should not continue to increase. Although the *average* weight of adults does rise through middle age, this is because appetite unfortunately holds up well while habits tend to become more sedentary. Adult forms of recreation are apt to involve watching others exert themselves. Time pressures, work and study responsibilities, concern with unrumpled coiffures and clothing and the unavailability of others having the same free hours and similar sports and dance preferences conspire to produce physical inertia. The palate also tends to become more sophisticated, and gourmet fare with its rich ingredients appeals more than simpler, less caloric meals.

There are, of course, glandular causes for overweight and emotional reasons for overeating, but glandular causes are not common. The excuse that one eats "like a bird" and that glands cause every mouthful to turn to fat is the most widespread of dietary self-delusions.

The soundest approach to weight control is to assess eating and exercise habits. *Habits* is the key word. It is essential to accustom oneself to the quantities and forms of food and the amounts and types of exercise that will maintain the desired weight.

SOME QUESTIONS AND ANSWERS

Speaking of self-delusions, now is a good time to find out whether you have accepted certain false ideas.

1. Should water intake be restricted while dieting? No, for thirst is a pretty good indication of the body's need for water. Dehydration results in a very temporary weight loss, but the loss is not of fat. Moreover, reduction of liquids is conducive to poor elimination of body wastes.
2. Should salt intake be restricted while dieting? Cutting out salt decreases water retention in the body. There are medically sound reasons for avoid-

ing large quantities, but the normal, healthy individual profits little by denying himself salt.

3. Is a gradual weight loss of a pound or two a week preferable to the "crash diet" approach? A crash diet may bring about temporary weight loss but leaves the appetite unimpaired. A gradual weight loss gives the body time to get used to lesser quantities of food and to make the new pattern of eating habitual.

4. Are vibratory machines and massage, or rolling and thumping the body helpful in shedding pounds? The body is passive in these processes and so burns few calories. Pounds can't be kneaded away or bounced off; they must be worked off.

5. Is eating between meals advisable while on a weight reduction schedule? Strangely enough, the dieter who eats small quantities frequently consumes less than the person who eats three meals only.

6. Does exercise increase appetite? Contrary to popular belief, research has shown that mild or moderate activity is an appetite depressant. Strenuous exercise increased appetite but was accompanied by weight loss (26) (15: 86).

7. Can spot reducing be accomplished through exercise and/or a drop in caloric intake? This question has a "yes" and "no" answer. For example, exercising the arms vigorously offers no guarantee that arm girth will be diminished. Individuals differ in their patterns of weight distribution and in the parts of the body that tend to lose or gain. Nevertheless, fat tends to be lost first from those areas where the most fat is deposited. Flabby tissues become firmed through use, and body contours thereby are improved. Added to this "spot" effect is the fact that a general weight loss usually reduces the size of disturbing body bulges more than it decreases girth in bony areas such as the hands, feet and head.

8. Are reducing pills an effective means of regulating eating habits? This is another question with two answers. When wisely prescribed by a reputable physician, pills may be helpful in easing the early stages of the dieting program. In part, they may serve as a psychological crutch. Still, contraindications for appetite depressants usually outweigh their benefits. If nothing else, the likelihood is great that the appetite will increase quickly to its previous level once the pills are discarded. The dispensing of weight control pills is one of the bag of tricks of the many charlatans who defraud the public. Some pills are utterly ineffective but harmless; others unfortunately contain ingredients potentially dangerous to the point of causing death.

9. Are there certain foods or combinations of foods which should be eaten exclusively while dieting for weight loss? Grapefruit, hard-boiled eggs, bananas, milk, cottage cheese and other specific foods are sometimes touted for their weight reduction powers. These are wholesome foods, but none has properties of peculiar value or provides in itself a well-balanced, long-term menu. One should eat as usual but in lesser quantity and with some change in the proportions of certain kinds of foods.

10. Does the word *dietetic* on the labels of food products mean "low calorie"? Careful reading of the fine print usually is necessary to find out in what

way a food so labeled is special. Most often an artificial sweetener is substituted for sugar or salt is omitted, and the latter does not cut calories. Sometimes fat content is lowered, but sugar content is so high that no caloric advantage is gained. In other instances, the caloric reduction is too insignificant to be meaningful.

11. Is a vegetarian diet advisable? The body requires an appropriate balance of proteins, carbohydrates, fats, minerals, and vitamins. It is almost impossible to obtain the vitamins and minerals needed without consuming animal products. With careful planning, meat can be eliminated if milk, eggs, cheese, dried peas, beans, lentils, and nuts are substituted.

Let us assume and hope that you will attack your weight problem through diet control and exercise. First set the number of pounds to be lost. Loss of 1 to 1½ pounds per week is a good rate, allowing satisfying progress and yet time for appetite adjustment. New eating habits are formed very slowly and there is seldom a long-term benefit from a crash program. Continual large fluctuations in weight from on-again-off-again dieting are physiologically inadvisable.

With a realistic short-term aim, you are ready to set your daily caloric limits and plan your exercise. For a weight loss of 1½ lbs./wk. you must decrease caloric intake and step up energy output to use 750 more calories per day than the body receives. The more vigorous the activity, the less you will have to curtail your diet. Adjustment now and then may be necessary if weight loss is too rapid or too slow. Plateaus are normal so do not be discouraged if you stay at the same level for several days.

THE DIET APPROACH

Although you can regulate your eating without counting calories, certain foods are deceptively high or low. Investment in an inexpensive booklet giving the calorie counts for foods is money well spent, for to change a pound in weight, you must eat 3,500 more or fewer calories than your body requires for the work it does. A chart showing the number of calories in common snack foods is in Appendix D, pages 93-94. Daily caloric requirements vary widely according to age, sex, metabolic rate and energy expended. A rough guess as to your own daily caloric needs can be found by multiplying your desired weight by fifteen. Increase the answer by one fourth if you are unusually active; decrease by one fourth if very sedentary. This rule of thumb takes no account of body framework or differences in metabolism. If you count your calories, you can soon determine the caloric requirement that is right for you.

The trick in dieting is to manage it without suffering too many pangs of hunger.

1. Choose bulky foods that take time to eat, such as tossed salad, carrot sticks and soup, so that the "hole" will be filled.
2. Deceive yourself about quantity by heaping a small plate rather than serving dabs on a dinner plate.
3. Use parsley, lemon slices and other garnishes. Arrange food attractively. Eye-appealing foods bring more satisfaction than drab plates.

4. Lean heavily on vegetables, fish and poultry and lightly on fatty meat, cheese, starches and sweets.
5. Use substitute foods. Replace whole with skim milk, coffee or whipping cream with an imitation vegetable product, cookies with graham crackers, etc.
6. Include dishes that you rate "fair." There is less temptation to overeat when foods are not favorites.
7. When you anticipate a large meal, give yourself shorter-than-usual rations for the other meals.
8. Eat small quantities five or six times a day in preference to a large meal at any time.
9. Take advantage of low caloric products displayed on dietetic shelves. Artificially sweetened soft drinks, jams, gelatin, ice cream, and fruits are generally available as are a variety of low-fat salad dressings. Numerous other more or less tasty items are also to be had. Frankly, most of these products are expensive, less flavorful and satisfying than regular foods, but the caloric advantage may be greater than the loss.
10. Avoid sauces, gravies, syrups, and other nonessentials, such as olives, dinner rolls, biscuits, preserves, or sour cream.
11. Be sure to include essential vitamins and minerals.
12. Remember your caloric allotment includes easily overlooked items such as snacks, butter, sugar, and catsup.

Consult several popular magazines. What good and bad weight control information can you find about diet, exercise, drugs, special appliances, or clothing?

EXERCISE A MUST

The exercise aspect of weight control is essential for everyone; for some, it may be adequate to insure success without dieting. Thinking about the importance of exercise in correcting overweight has undergone modification in recent years. Experts used to point out the number of miles to be walked, stairs to be climbed or hours to be spent doing housework in order to dispose of a single pound of body weight. It requires, for example, about thirty-five hours of walking to use the calories represented by a pound of fat. The magnitude of the task is tiring even to contemplate!

What the experts previously overlooked was that excess poundage is rarely acquired by overindulging to the extent of 3,500 extra calories at one sitting, and neither must it be lost at such a rate. Usually one develops a state of plumpness almost imperceptibly. Even sixty-five calories per day above the energy expended, perhaps an extra slice of bread, add up to a one-pound weight gain in about two months.

On the other hand, the simple exercise of walking rapidly consumes approximately four calories per minute for a 117-pound person. By spending an otherwise sedentary fifteen minutes of your day in walking you can afford an extra slice of bread; by foregoing the bread, you can painlessly lose an ounce every few days. The more exercise, especially if combined with dietary restriction, the larger the dividends. Note that in trying to lose weight, the total amount of work done is what counts, not the circulorespiratory demands. An hour's walk ten minutes at a time is as much work as walking for 60 minutes without stopping. Calories are burned more quickly at heavier and more slowly at lighter body weights.

The physically active individual who overeats gains relatively less because the extra calories are to some degree offset by the increased energy required to move the body. A sedentary overeater simply accumulates fat since he fails to expend energy in moving about.

The exercise aspect of conditioning for weight loss is easy to plan: expend energy at a rate in keeping with your purposes and current state of fitness. Consult the table in Appendix C, pages 88-92 for the calories burned per minute by participation in various sports, dance, and calisthenics. Be sure to count actual participation only. Waiting for a turn and rest periods require very little energy.

1. If you enjoy a strenuous activity, it can be your chief means of using up energy. Skiing, field sports, basketball, squash, badminton singles, modern, folk, or square dance are among the excellent choices.
2. You can participate alone, without special equipment or facilities, in jogging, running in place, jumping rope, and calisthenics.
3. Select also exercises in which you work against resistance. Jumping, hopping, and stair climbing are good because the body weight is lifted in each.

SAMPLE PROGRAM OF CONDITIONING

I. Goals
   A. Long-term: to lose 10 pounds, from 143 to 133, and to firm muscles.
   B. Short-term: to lose 1½ pounds the first week.
II. Assessment of Usual Day-to-Day Activities
   A. Custom of playing tennis twice a week helps some with firming process but has not been adequate to keep weight down.
   B. Needed are a reduction in diet and additional exercise to equivalent of 750 calories per day or 5,250 per week.
III. Conditioning Program for One Week
   A. Diet   Cal. Loss/Week
      Substitute skim for whole milk at lunch   567
      Substitute artificial sweetener for 3 tsp. sugar in 2 cups
         coffee per day   210
      Substitute low calorie soda pop for one with sugar each
         afternoon   723
      Substitute fresh fruit, gelatin, ice milk, etc. for cake,
         pie and rich puddings (5 days)   710
      Skip customary midmorning doughnut (5 days)   980

Skip 1 slice bread and butter (7 days)   630
Restrict food selections and/or limit usual quantities by
  approximately 100 more calories (7 days); usual total
  per day was about 2,200; it now is about 1,565   700
B. Exercise (Swimming and Calisthenics)
  1. 20 minute swim, mixed strokes (3 days) at 5.7 cal./min. 342
  2. Calisthenics 14 minutes (5 days) at 5½ cal./min.
     and ½ minute stationary running, 70 steps left foot   385
     at 23.2 calories per minute   55
                                          TOTAL 5,302

Do series twice without rest between exercises. Exercises are described in Appendix A.

Approximate Time	Exercise	Number of Executions
30 seconds	Jumping Jills	12
30 seconds	Back Leg Lift	10 each leg
30 seconds	Curl Sit-Ups	12
1 minute	Ski Stretch	6
1 minute	Squat Thrust Jump	6
·1 minute	Hip Lift	3
1 minute	V Sit	6
30 seconds	Thigh Trimmer	10 each leg
30 seconds	Push-Ups	12
30 seconds	Waltz Time Swing	4

Conditioning for fitness

8

"Fitness" in its broadest sense denotes an all-encompassing state of positive well-being. Mental, social, emotional, and physical good health are implied as are motor skills and all qualities describing the best manner of living. The connotation in everyday usage, however, refers to the possession of such elements as muscular strength, muscular endurance, flexibility, circulorespiratory endurance, agility, and power (work per unit of time). Isotonic exercise is necessary for their development and may be supplemented with the isometric form. Weight training, aerobics, calisthenics, sports, and dance and many other forms of activity are suitable ways of developing the qualities of general fitness.

TESTING YOUR PRESENT STATUS

As you begin your program you may wish to test yourself on several fitness components. Numerous tests and performance standards are available for cir-culorespiratory fitness and motor fitness (19:153-154) (32:344-350) (7:136) (35). It may be fun to try some of these cited tests and to compare your scores with the standards, but all that is really needed for general fitness purposes is that you use your own scores as a basis for measuring your progress on a few informal representative tests.

Quick Stand—Circulorespiratory anaerobic response and agility (including elements of muscular endurance, flexibility, and power).

Preliminary to the test Stand with your side to the wall and make a chalk line at the level of your normal upward reach. Then put the chalk aside and sit down on the floor. After two minutes, have your partner count your pulse for the next 20 seconds and record the score.

Test   Start lying flat on your back on the floor. At the signal "GO" stand up to touch the chalk mark (or almost) and then lie back down to touch your shoulders to the floor. Repeat as many times as possible in 30 seconds. Your partner counts and records the total score. Count 1 as you crouch, 2 at full reach to the chalk line, 3 when you sit and 4 as the shoulders touch the floor. At the signal "Stop" immediately sit on the floor. Ten seconds are then allowed for your partner to locate your pulse. Then at the signal "Go" the partner counts your radial pulse for 20 seconds, multiplies the figure by 3 and records the result as your pulse rate for one minute. Note that the pulse is taken by holding the fingers, not the thumb, against the radial artery close to the juncture of the wrist and thumb. If this pulse is difficult to count, the fingers may be held gently against the carotid artery in the neck.

Sitting Reach (15:145-146)—Trunk Flexibility

Preliminary to the Test   Place a box about 15 inches high or a bench on its side against the wall or use the first step of folding bleachers for an upright surface. Tape a yardstick to the top at a right angle to the wall and with six or eight inches projecting forward over the edge of the step, box, or bench.

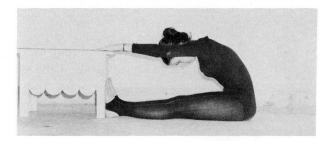

Fig. 6   Trunk Flexibility Test

Test   Start in long sitting position facing the wall with the soles of the feet flat against the vertical surface. Slowly slide the fingers forward on the yardstick as far as possible and hold for three seconds. Your score is the distance of your fingertips in inches from the edge of the vertical surface. Reaches short of the edge are recorded as minus scores and those beyond the edge as positive numbers.

Curl Sit-Ups—Muscular Endurance of Abdominal Muscles

Start in a supine position, hands clasped behind your head, knees bent to about a 65-degree angle and feet held flat on the floor by your partner. At the signal "Go" curl up, head leading, to touch the elbows to the knees. Immediately curl back down. Repeat as many times as possible for one minute. Your partner records the number of sit-ups performed by counting each touch of elbows to knees or touch of head to floor as 1/2 point.

Knee Push-Ups—Muscular Endurance of Arms and Shoulders

Start lying prone on a mat with legs together and lower legs raised toward the ceiling, and palms on the floor by the shoulders. At the signal "Go" push to lift the body from the knees until your arms are straight. Then reverse direction to touch the head or chest to the floor. Repeat as many times as possible for 30 seconds. Your partner records the number of push-ups performed by counting each full arm extension or each dip to the floor as 1/2 point.

THE WEIGHT TRAINING ROUTE

A systematic program of weight training in which the resistance against which work is performed is progressively increased places emphasis on muscular strength, muscular endurance, and flexibility.

Equipment suitable for home (or gymnasium) use includes barbells, dumbbells, a low bench, horizontal bar, and an incline board.

A weight training practice session starts with a preliminary warm-up with calisthenics principally for stretching. This is followed by a series of exercises performed in sets. A set is a number of consecutive executions of an exercise at a given weight or resistance. If more than one set of the same exercise is to be done, a rest of several minutes intervenes.

Keep in Mind:

1. Select exercises according to the muscle groups involved and the strengthening, muscular endurance, or stretching effect desired.
2. For muscle strengthening and stretching, work with resistances that can be managed for about 6-10 executions of the exercise.
3. For muscle endurance, lessen the resistance so that you can do about 20 executions.
4. Be sure to use good body mechanics (see chapter 3) to avoid injury to weak muscle groups.
5. Alternate practice between three and four times per week, if possible, and continue the same program until you feel you can handle a heavier load.
6. The order of exercises should allow fatigued muscle groups to rest before working again.

Representative weight training exercises are described in Appendix A, pages 71-85. The series is for beginners and for strengthening purposes should be performed against resistances that can be handled easily for the number of executions suggested.

THE AEROBICS ROUTE[1]

The primary goal of the aerobics program of exercise developed by Dr. Kenneth Cooper, originally for Air Force men, is to improve circulorespiratory

[1]Material in this section was condensed from two books (7) (8).

endurance. Other elements of overall fitness may benefit depending on choice of activity. The basic idea of the program is to progress in quantity and strenuousness of aerobic exercise until you can earn a given number of points per week. Points are based on oxygen consumed during various types, speeds, and amounts of exercise. For example: Bicycling three miles in 12-17 minutes = 1 point; one set of tennis = 1½ points; 30 minutes of skiing (no lift or wait time) = 3 points. According to Dr. Cooper, 20-24 points are sufficient for maintenance of fitness in women.

A medical examination within the year for women under 30 years of age and the absence of conditions restricting exercise are prerequisite to following the entire plan. If you have been exercising regularly at least three times per week for the past six weeks, you may want to start your program by taking the 12 Minute Test or the 1½ Mile Test. If you have not been exercising regularly you should not test yourself but proceed instead to a conditioning program designed for your age group. Aerobics Starter Programs for running, walking, rope skipping, stair climbing, swimming, bicycling, and stationary cycling are described.

When you achieve a rating of Good or Excellent in endurance, you may design your own program to add up to 20-24 points per week by consulting the charts that give point values for various sports and dance activities as well as for the Starter Program activities.

12 Minute Test

Your score on the test is the distance you can comfortably cover by running and walking for a 12-minute period of time. Most tracks are one-fourth of a mile around and are marked to indicate distances. Prior to the test, warm up for about four minutes with stretching exercises and easy walking and jogging.

Classification on the test for women under 30 years of age is as follows: Very Poor—less than .95 miles; Poor—.95-1.14 miles; Fair—1.15-1.34 miles; Good—1.35-1.64 miles; Excellent—1.65 miles or more.

1½ Mile Test

Your score on the test is the time taken in minutes and seconds to run 1½ miles. Warm up before starting as for the 12 Minute Test. Classification for women under 30 years of age is as follows: Very Poor—17:30+; Poor—17:30-15:31; Fair—15:30-13:01; Good—13:00-11:16; Excellent—11:16 or less.

Following Cooper's Aerobics Plan

In order to follow the Aerobics conditioning plan you should consult *Aerobics for Women* by Mildred and Kenneth Cooper (8) or *The New Aerobics* by Kenneth Cooper (7).

THE SPORTS AND DANCE ROUTE

Contributions of various sports and dance forms to fitness differ markedly. The training effects are not only specific in terms of the abilities developed but specific to the parts of the body involved. By analyzing the activities you have in mind, you can select combinations that will help you toward motor and circulorespiratory fitness.

Field sports, badminton and tennis singles, aerobic dance, folk and square dance, paddleball, and skiing are examples of good choices for improvement of circulorespiratory endurance. Flexibility, strength, agility, and power are essentials in gymnastics, ballet, and modern dance. Arm and shoulder strength are emphasized in archery, canoeing, rowing, and competitive swimming. You can add many others to these lists.

Since sports involving an implement tend to be one-sided, supplementary activity is needed to provide balanced development. Specific exercises for the abdominal muscles may be important, also, for few sports and dance forms put heavy demands on this part of the body.

Participation in your chosen activities should occur at least three times per week. You will have to use judgment as to time and frequency according to the strenuousness of the activity. There must be a good workout demanding strength, flexibility, agility, and power if you are to raise your motor fitness level. To improve circulorespiratory endurance, remember that the heart rate should be increased at least 60 percent of the range between resting rate and maximum rate. Exercise at a steady pace or alternating between sprints of more intense spurts and intervals of less exertion should continue for a minimum of 20-30 minutes.

THE CALISTHENICS ROUTE

A program of calisthenics as a means of improving fitness is a popular choice of many people who lack time, opportunity, or inclination to engage in other forms of exercise. An added advantage lies in the ease with which one can ensure a work-out by all major muscle groups. Strength, flexibility, and muscular endurance are readily increased through calisthenics, but circulorespiratory endurance and agility are often overlooked. Rope jumping, running in place, and stair climbing are good supplements for endurance purposes. Agility is fostered by quick changes in body position and direction of movement.

Several interesting progressions of exercise are available. One is the President's Council on Physical Fitness Program for Women (28) which includes orientation exercises followed by programs at five levels of difficulty. Another is the Royal Canadian Air Force Plan for Women, called the XBX program (30). This is a more detailed plan than the first. There are four charts of ten exercises each and twelve levels of performance within each chart. The number of executions of each exercise that must be completed within a set time increases from level to level. Recommendations as to how far to try to progress toward the forty-eighth level are made for different age groups.

By referring to Appendix C, can you design a personal fitness program that will fit into your weekly schedule and meet these requirements: expenditure of about 750 calories per week and improvement of circulorespiratory endurance?

If you prefer to develop your own series, choose exercises for the arms and shoulder girdle, abdomen, back, trunk, legs, and feet and supplement with vigorous locomotor activities. Always start your series with warm-up exercises: bending, stretching, arm swinging, etc. Include variety in direction of movement and pace and incorporate exercises that develop each component of physical fitness.

Be imaginative but subject your ideas to thoughtful evaluation before you proceed. Err in the direction of too little work at the start. Remember then to progress at a slow, steady pace. Exercise at a level that pushes you a bit but doesn't leave you completely exhausted or with painfully sore muscles. Within the period, include at least one-half to one minute of running in place, rope jumping, jogging, or other circulorespiratory endurance exercise. Increase this time gradually to five minute bouts.

Do your same program daily if possible, three times per week at a minimum. Continue until you feel comfortable performing the series without rest between exercises. Then periodically step up the intensity of the program by choosing different exercises, adapting the same exercises, increasing the number of executions, doing more in the same length of time or some combination of these procedures.

Conditioning for sports and dance participation

9

When devising a conditioning program for a particular sport or dance form, there are three approaches, all of which should be utilized. First, practice of the specific elements of the sport or dance is, in itself, a conditioning process that promotes improved performance. Secondly, weight training, circulorespiratory endurance activities, and calisthenics can develop the strength and flexibility in the muscle groups and joints directly involved in a particular activity and provide the endurance needed. Such fundamental procedures prepare the body to be accurate, forceful, controlled and yet free in its movement.

The demands imposed by conditioning exercise should match closely those of the sport or dance for which you are preparing. The muscles should have to apply the greatest force in exercise at the same angles as they do in the activity. The spacing and duration of work and of rest should be as they are under game or dance conditions. Often an interval training program can be designed to approximate the pacing and load desired.

Also to be regarded as possible conditioning exercises are activities in which there are similar patterns of movement. A tennis serve and a badminton overhead high clear are specific neuromuscular coordinations, yet there are common transferable elements. The tennis player who has engaged in badminton all winter will find his tennis game benefited to the extent that he has gained in arm, shoulder-girdle and abdominal strength, eye-hand coordination and the like. Even the spatial pattern described by the racket arm, the placement of the feet, and the point of racket contact with the object are sufficiently alike to permit a conscious transfer of intellectual comprehension and kinesthetic awareness.

Begin training for a sport about a month ahead of the season to get your muscles and circulorespiratory systems into a ready state. The conditioning program is best mapped out in several progressive phases culminating, if possible, in exercise which makes demands above the level normally called for in the sport for which you are preparing. When participation in the sport itself is begun, the conditioning program per se should be tapered off and become supplementary. At this stage you may do conditioning exercise at intervals between or in lieu of scheduled sports practices when weather or other circumstances interfere.

SELECTED CONDITIONING EXERCISES FOR SPORTS AND DANCE
(For exercise descriptions, refer to Appendix A)

FOR GENERAL WARM-UP
Exercises 1, 10, 13, 22, 34

All running games and sports
Dance
Gymnastics
Skiing

FOR ABDOMINAL STRENGTH
Exercises 6, 21, 27, 32, 40, 45

All sports and dance

FOR LEG STRENGTH
Exercises 9, 27, 29, 33, 38, 41, 42, 47

All running games and sports
Aquatics
Cycling
Dance
Fencing
Gymnastics
Riding
Skiing
Volleyball

FOR SHOULDER GIRDLE FLEXIBILITY OR RELAXATION
Exercises 1, 34, 35, 40

All racket sports and ball games
Aquatics
Archery
Dance
Fencing
Gymnastics

FOR TRUNK OR HAMSTRING FLEXIBILITY
Exercises 12, 19, 21, 25, 27, 30, 43

All ball games
Aquatics
Dance
Gymnastics
Riding
Skiing

FOR TAPERING OFF
Exercises 8, 18, 19, 34

All racket sports and ball games
All running games and sports
Dance
Gymnastics
Skiing

FOR ARM AND SHOULDER GIRDLE STRENGTH
Exercises 4, 11, 25, 26, 27, 36, 37, 39, 40, 44, 46

All racket sports and ball games
Aquatics
Archery
Boating
Gymnastics
Riding

FOR FOOTWORK
Exercises 14, 15, 22, 23, 24, 28, 31, 38

All racket sports and ball games
All running or jumping games or sports
Dance
Fencing

FOR BACK AND HIP STRENGTH
Exercises 2, 3, 8, 16, 26

All sports and dance

FOR CIRCULORESPIRATORY ENDURANCE (if continued long enough)
Exercises 22, 23, 24

Aquatics
Badminton
Basketball
Cycling
Field Sports
Skiing
Squash
Track

Conditioning for poise in standing and sitting

10

Poise is the outward expression of inner confidence. Posture and body movement denote poise when they are appropriate to the occasion, seemingly effortless and in no way distracting. The skills needed to stand and sit gracefully and to move into these positions can be acquired; their mastery fosters self-assurance.

STANDING

In view of the very limited amount of time that most of us spend standing bolt upright and stock still, it may seem somewhat ridiculous to attempt to mold oneself into a silhouette that conforms to the *ideal* standing posture. The tiresome term *posture* and the even more tiresome admonitions to assume a good standing position have aroused somewhat negative, if not downright rebellious, attitudes in the young of each generation.

Why so much stress on an erect stance? Does it really matter how one stands? Is the same position best for everyone?

Why Good Posture?   One reason that standing posture has been emphasized, though not a very good one, is that it presents a concept we can grasp. We can see a stationary position, judge it and even measure it; the body in motion, however, shifts continually from one attitude to another.

It has been claimed also that maintenance of the ideal posture is less fatiguing than any alternative, a myth that has been perpetuated. The standard posture requires more effort than certain other less erect postures.

After this negative approach, you may be ready to heave a sigh of relief and forget the whole problem. This would be short-sighted, for a balanced standing position offers real values that can be yours for the cultivating.

One of the immediate and most important dividends of good carriage is its effect on appearance. Straight lines are slenderizing, but the thinnest figure looks thick and dumpy through the middle when posture is poor. A thrust-forward head and shoulders and hollow lower back form an unattractive con-tour that draws attention away from whatever assets their owner possesses.

Clothing looks better if posture is balanced, for even straight seams and hems hang crooked when the wearer has lopsided habits and body outlines. If one customarily stands with a hip thrust out or with the head far forward, a protective fatty pad tends to develop over the one hip joint or between the shoulders at the base of the neck.

It is on those occasions when we stand still that we often want to look our best, our most poised, and graceful. Anyone who appears on a platform, speaks before a group, attends a stand-up social affair, or applies for a job is in the public eye. Because posture tends to mirror feelings, an awkward or careless stance is often interpreted as a reflection of lazy, don't-care, or inept patterns of behavior, and often the first impression determines whether there is to be a longer acquaintance.

Poor posture can and does cause certain stresses and strains that may cause trouble now or lead to discomfort in later years. Foot trouble, for example, may result from poor foot mechanics. Lower back fatigue or pain may be posture-related and often is associated with weak abdominal muscles. Knee injury is more likely to occur if the knees are habitually hyperextended. In the back-knee position, there is no shock-absorbing backward motion possible if the joint is struck from the front and thus no margin of safety as there is when the knee is slightly relaxed. One-sided habits may lead to lateral curvature of the spine. Because of the unequal muscle tension on the two sides of a laterally curved spine, muscle strain and pain may occur.

During pregnancy and in the years when mothers must lift and carry small children who daily grow larger and heavier, a well-balanced standing position and good body mechanics in general assume more importance than usual. Maintaining good balance while pregnant is difficult as the weight of the child displaces the center of gravity forward. It is necessary to rock back on the heels to compensate for the changed distribution of weight without hollowing the back.

Four-footed creatures do not have standing posture problems, and they get along very nicely without posture instruction or corrective exercises. Man, unfortunately, is poorly designed to stand upright. The feet form a very small base on which to mount relatively long legs, a flexible spine insecurely sup-ported and a heavy head. Human habits contribute to the difficulties too. Driving an automobile, reading, engaging in certain sports, and doing house-work or gardening tend to draw our heads forward, the better to see, and our trunks toward the hands, the better to manipulate objects. Standing posture, for man, is a skill acquired only after many trials and numerous tumbles.

The Ideal Posture   What is good standing posture? It is a position in which the body segments are well-balanced and firmly supported, giving an overall appearance of erectness and ease. The "ideal" standing posture, as we now describe it, was apparently conceived of by Braune and Fischer in the last century. They were not attempting to set a posture standard, but they rea-soned that a stance in which the center of gravity of each body segment falls

Start with number 1, your base of support, and follow these checkpoints.

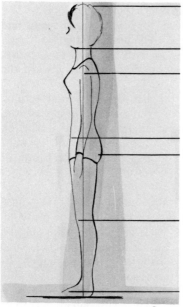

7. A feeling of elevation and extension from feet to head, but with sufficient relaxation to avoid a rigid look.

6. Chin tucked in, head level.

5. Shoulders level and easy, chest high.

4. Abdomen flat or almost so, and lower back (lumbar) curve moderate.

3. Hips tucked under, that is, the pelvis tilted up in front and down in back.

2. Knees easy, not locked back, and knee caps pointed straight ahead. You may need to rotate the knees outward slightly to achieve this position.

1. Toes straight ahead; feet 2 to 3 inches apart; weight evenly balanced on both heels; along the outer borders, and all across the balls of the feet; ankles directly above the feet so that the ankle bones don't protrude inward. Heel cords straight.

Fig. 7   Ideal Standing Posture

directly above the one below affords a convenient posture from which to measure deviations. Although other postures, such as the military bearing for men and the exaggerated lumbar curve once decreed by fashion for women, have served as models from time to time, it is the vertically aligned standing position that has gained universal acceptance as the correct posture. Seen from the side view, a perpendicular line falls through the tip of the ear, the axis of the shoulder, hip and knee joint, and the center of the ankle.

Ideal posture is a guide, but each individual must adapt the pattern to his own basic body build. For some, absolute conformance to the standard results in a stiff, unnatural pose. This is not to say, however, that whatever is comfortable is all right. It does take effort to maintain an acceptable body alignment, but there has been in the past too great an emphasis on urging everyone to conform exactly to the same mold.

How many one-sided habits can you think of that tend to result in carrying one shoulder lower than the other? Are any of these related to right or left hand preference?

The best conditioning program for attaining your own ideal posture is to model your basic position after the standard one, check it in the mirror or have someone check it for you, and then settle for the closest reasonably comfortable approximation you can attain after *concentrated* practice. Any change in your habitual stance will feel strange at first so don't decide you have found what is right for you until it also looks attractive and well-balanced.

There are three prerequisites without which the attainment of a good standing posture is impossible. If these are met, it is rare, indeed, for any normal young person to fail to learn the necessary skills. The three essentials are:

1. An honest desire and determined intent to stand well.
2. An understanding of the essentials of good carriage.
3. An ability to assume the correct body positions and to feel the relationships of the body segments to one another.

You should assume an erect yet relaxed carriage many times a day. Gradually the kinesthetic feel of the position will become automatic.

Looking Glass Test   Whenever you look into a mirror check your alignment from toes up to the head. Concentrate on the kinesthetic awareness, the "feel" of the body parts when held in proper relation to one another. As you step away from the mirror, hold your erect position as long as you can remember to do so.

Back to the Wall   Between mirror checks, back up to a flat wall to help find a balanced posture. The head, shoulders, hips, calves, and heels should touch the wall. The space in the lower back area should accommodate the fingers but not the palms. As you become more kinesthetically conscious of body position you will be able to assume a good stance by imagining that you must squeeze yourself sideways through a very narrow space.

CHECKLIST FOR STANDING POSTURE

Ask a partner to evaluate your standing posture from the side and back views. A ✔ should be marked in the Correct column if the position meets the standard. If there is a fault, the degree should be noted by writing "1" for slight, "2" for moderate and "3" for marked.

This all-at-once approach makes sense because postural faults occur in groups. When something zigs there must be a corresponding zag. The most usual combination of errors is forward head and shoulders, hollow back (incorrect pelvic tilt), locked knees, and pronation. One low shoulder, usually the right, also is often seen. Other lateral deviations which cause asymmetrical contours are not unusual but are less amenable to change through a conditioning program.

C Shape to T Shape   Another technique for eliminating several postural errors all at once often works for those with a C-shaped silhouette. They have locked their knees and let the midriff slide forward to lead the body. The trick is to hold the head and feet stationary while imagining that someone has poked a finger in the midriff to push it back to a centered position between the head and the feet. The new stance is apt to cause a toppling forward sensation owing to the long-standing habit of leaning back from the hips. A sideways look at a mirror or a check by a friend will assure you that you are truly vertical.

Correct		Faults	
Side View			
Head and Neck	Erect	Forward	Backward
Shoulders	Balanced and Relaxed	Forward	Thrust backward
Upper Back	Normal curve	Too rounded	Too flat
Chest	Normally lifted	Low	Too high
Abdomen	Contracted	Protruding	
Lumbar Curve	Normal curve	Hollow	Too flat
Knees	Easy	Hyperextended	Too flexed
Back View			
Head and Neck	Erect	Tilted left	Tilted right
Shoulders	Level	Low left	Low right
Hips	Level	High left	High right
Ankles	Straight	Pronated	Supinated
Feet	Parallel	Toes out	Toes in

Part by Part Exercise   Although the musculature of the normal college student is seldom too weak or too contracted to permit assumption of a balanced stance, strengthening and limbering exercises which focus on particular faults may help. If nothing else they serve as a kinesthetic reminder to bring the body segments into line. The exercises noted under each fault are representative of movements that encourage good alignment. See Appendix A for descriptions.

Forward Head and Neck: Nos. 2, 33.
Forward Shoulders: Nos. 2, 25, 35, 36, 39.
Relaxed Abdomen: Nos. 6, 17, 40, 45.
Hollow Back: Nos. 6, 17, 21.

SITTING

You might think of sitting postures as falling into formal and informal categories. Find a spot to sit and plop into it on casual, at-home occasions, but when you prefer the poised and less conspicuous approach, there are better techniques. Big, soft chairs are fine for taking your ease. Don't worry about the effects on posture as long as you are comfortable and the lower back is supported. When appearances matter, straight chairs are more suitable and are simpler to get in and out of.

Being Seated   Choose your chair and approach it directly. As you draw near adapt your stride so that on the last step the forward leg almost touches the chair. Do a reverse turn on the balls of the feet ending with the calf of one leg against the chair seat. Now you know the chair is there without peering over your shoulder. From this forward stride position, lower yourself by bending the knees while keeping the trunk erect. Avoid using your hands to

Imagine yourself with an armload of books making your way along a crowded row of chairs like this one. By considering the principles of sitting and getting up gracefully, can you demonstrate a good way to get into and out of the chair?

help. Once you are down, stay where you are for a few moments. If the chair is large and your position must be adjusted, do so by placing a hand on the seat to brace as you move. This is more graceful than pushing on the arms of the chair with your elbows poked out.

Hands in the lap or one forearm on the chair arm is recommended, for resting on both chair arms simultaneously has a widening effect on the body appearance.

Several foot and leg positions are comfortable and attractive. Feet and knees close together, one foot slightly in the lead is always good. Ankles crossed or feet together and both legs slanted to one side also presents a slender body position since the calves are narrowed in the eyes of the viewer. If you cross your knees do so by sliding one over the other so that the legs retain contact with each other as you move. Cross above rather than at the knee joint to avoid having the top leg hang at an awkward angle. It is best not to cross the knees at all when you are seated on a platform unless you are wearing a full and long dress or a pant outfit.

Shun these positions on company occasions: toes up, heels resting on the floor; feet twisted around the chair legs; knees apart; feet parallel and squarely placed on the floor. The last is mechanically good but not flattering to the leg line.

The hips should rest against the back of a straight chair for best support. The chair is too large for you if you cannot slide all the way back and yet place the soles of the feet on the floor.

Sitting on the floor is an informal posture. Still, there are better and poorer ways of going about it. Perhaps the easiest is to drop to both knees. From there sit back on the lower legs and insteps or, instead, swing the hips sideways and let yourself down onto them as you brace with one hand on the floor. A long sitting position, legs straight out in front, leaning or not on the hands, is reasonably graceful. Other postures are acceptable when you are dressed suitably and are not concerned with looking your best, but a slumped attitude is never attractive or mechanically good.

Standing From a Sitting Position   When seated in a straight chair, touch the ball of one foot under the front of the chair and place the other foot slightly forward, sole flat on the floor. With a little forward hip lean, you should be able to rise by extending the knees. The back remains erect. There is no need to use the hands to push off from the chair arms or to swing your arms forward in the process. Either action is angular and ungraceful. If the seat is very deep and low and so constructed that you cannot tuck one foot underneath, you may have to use your hands and arms to help lift the body. If so, place the palms on the seat and push as the knees straighten. This is less clumsy than hauling oneself up from the chair arms.

The key factors in standing up smoothly or in sitting down are to keep the back reasonably straight, the hips under the body, and the arms close to the sides. With these points in mind you should be able to work out appropriate ways of rising from the floor as well as from a chair or couch.

In and Out of an Automobile   Automobiles, especially sports cars, challenge the ingenuity when it comes to the mechanics of entrances and exits. The principles for other sitting arrangements also apply here. One tries to keep the body movement compact, the legs reasonably close together, and the hips low.

Open the front door, face the front bumper, then sit. Now swing both legs into the car simultaneously. In exiting, reverse the procedure by placing the feet on the ground before you stand. Above all, avoid entering an automobile head first, bent over with the hips high. Also avoid getting in or out by swinging one leg only so that you are momentarily seated with one foot inside, knees wide apart, and one foot on the ground pointed out at a right angle to the seat. When entering or leaving the back seat, bend the knees and keep the hips low.

In and Out of a Room   Have you ever opened the door of a room where a group was assembled only to have conversation cease and to find all eyes focused on your entrance? This is one of those awkward moments when you long for invisibility.

The situation can be turned to your advantage if you retain outward composure and make several deliberate well-calculated moves. First, prepare before you burst into a room by grasping the door handle with one hand, the right hand for doors hinged at your right and vice versa. Open the door, step through and let the hand slide from the outer to the inner handle. As you retain your grip on the handle, which now is behind you, slowly and gently close the door without turning to look at it. Use this pause to glance around the room, size up the situation, and decide exactly where you wish to go. The brief hesitation keeps you from starting off at random only to find that there are no empty seats or acquaintances in the direction you have taken.

No special skills are demanded in forming appropriate sitting habits. The conditioning, or in this case habituating, process is a matter of repeated practice of the movements called for under different circumstances until you can perform them smoothly and inconspicuously.

A REMINDER

The formality of the occasion, your location in relation to those who observe you, and your clothing are to be considered whether you are standing or sitting. In all situations, positions in which the body lines are relatively straight and simple are more attractive than angular, zigzag, or twisted postures.

Conditioning for efficiency in walking and running

11

The locomotor skills of walking and running are closely related and yet different in purpose, timing, and execution. One or the other is vital to almost every aspect of daily living. Both are excellent forms of conditioning for fitness, sports, and dance because of their total body involvement. On the other hand, these activities may, themselves, be the ends toward which your conditioning program is directed.

WALKING

For most of us, walking is a matter of putting one foot ahead of the other, a means of getting somewhere. We have practiced daily for years, and our gait has become a fixed part of self-identity. We recognize acquaintances at a distance by the manner in which they move, and we discriminate easily between graceful and awkward walking motions. We are less perceptive in evaluating our own gait.

The Walk to Notice   We tend to judge personality in part by body movement. A poor walk may amuse, distract, annoy, or even offend an observer. A good walk is harmonious and aesthetically appealing. A good walk is individual, stylized by the particular walker, and dependent in part upon his body size, proportions, and temperament. Matters of environment such as terrain, temperature, wind, and footwear interact with personal qualities. Nevertheless, the basic elements of a good walking gait are identifiable.

1. An attractive gait is always superimposed on an erect standing posture in which the body weight is shifted forward slightly from the ankles.
2. The leg swing is started at the hip and motion is forward with a minimum of lateral or vertical movement.
3. The feet are pointed straight ahead and are placed just to the left and right of an imaginary center line.

4. The toes are used actively for the push-off of each step.
5. The arms are swung freely and naturally but shoulders remain level and parallel.
6. The body weight is eased onto the supporting foot to minimize noise and landing shock.
7. The stride is moderate in length.
8. Even rhythm and controlled relaxation are evident.

Walks to Avoid   Several stereotyped and ungainly walking patterns can be seen in any crowd. Some are labeled more masculine or more feminine in character and are especially noticeable if practiced by the noncorresponding sex. The following list is by no means complete.

1. Long stride, exaggerated arm swing; opposite shoulder moves forward with each step.
2. Short steps, little leg action above the knee.
3. Entire body weight rolls from side to side; feet may separate laterally by 3 or more inches.
4. Pelvis leads the body, and upper trunk leans backward.
5. Lateral hip thrust; body weight shifts toward the side of the supporting leg.
6. Body weight transferred too soon so that walker clumps.
7. Toes pointed out.

Walking Under Adverse Circumstances   High heels and platform soles belong at the head of the adverse circumstances list. For one thing, the usually thinner sole of high heeled shoes is tiring on hard surfaces. Worse yet, the narrow heel and sole decrease the size of the base. Balance is precarious on a small base and even more so on a slanting support. This threat to safety is doubled by numerous chinks and crevices in sidewalks and streets which can trip the unwary heel. Platform soles share with other high heels serious disadvantages. Any surface unevenness such as a small pebble under a shoe causes the foot to tip laterally and the ankle to abduct or adduct (tilt out or in). This ankle movement is magnified when the foot is elevated above the ground and the probability of a sprain is increased. The platform sole is also a hazard in driving an automobile. The foot must be lifted higher to move from gas pedal to brake, a more time consuming act than with the usual shoe, and sensitivity to pressure from the gas and brake pedals is lessened by the thick sole.

It takes practice to walk well in high heels, but the necessary adaptations may be readily understood. The body weight must be shifted backward at the ankles to compensate for the forward tilt of the feet. The stride should be shortened and the step be a flat-footed one rather than a heel-toe sequence. The higher the heel and the faster the walk, the more exaggerated the necessary modifications.

To walk anywhere in a great hurry is to proceed under another adverse circumstance. Efficient and reasonably graceful action can be achieved only by lengthening the stride while simultaneously bending the knees more than usual. The essential increase in forward lean tends to occur in the trunk instead of in the ankle unless the walker takes care to avoid a bent body position.

Walking up and down stairs has its own built-in problems. Aside from the question of fatigue, the walker must concern himself with safety and appearance. Safety recommendations include keeping the hand lightly on the railing and placing the whole foot on each stair tread. Aesthetic pitfalls are numerous. Hauling oneself up by the hand rail is number one; toeing out in a ducklike position is another. Skipping steps is good conditioning practice but recommended only for the most informal of occasions. The walker should angle both feet slightly in the same sideward direction on stair treads too narrow to accommodate the full foot in a straight forward position.

Earth Shoes have been promoted by shoe manufacturers as being restful to the feet and beneficial to foot function. Further investigation is needed to determine conclusively the effects of this type of footwear. Research by Scherer (31) indicates that Earth Shoes may be helpful in relieving certain conditions including bunions and hammer toe but may be contraindicated in the presence of diabetes or peripheral vascular or neurological disease. Most wearers of Earth Shoes experience some discomfort during the first week or two, and many podiatrists do not recommend them.

The choice of footwear for exercise is important because the stress on the feet and ankles is increased markedly by such locomotor activities as running and jumping; by quick starts, stops and turns; and by the addition of external weights to the body. Shoes should have good arch support, soft, cushiony innersoles, and thick, soft soles.

If your interest in walking extends to hiking, backpacking, or orienteering, a conditioning program is in order. Practice should occur three to five times a week if possible. Conditioning for fitness and exercise for the development of muscular endurance in the legs, back, and shoulders will be helpful.

1. Find your starting level by walking for a mile at a moderate pace (about 2 miles/hour if sedentary; 110-120 steps/minute if usually active). Note the time taken and whether you are fatigued.
2. Gradually increase your work load by walking farther and at a faster pace.
3. Practice on the level and over rough and hilly terrain.
4. Walk carrying a backpack. Gradually add items to the pack to increase the workload.
5. Engage in activities involved in conditioning for fitness, chapter 8.
6. Engage in isotonic exercise, either weight lifting or calisthenics to improve muscular endurance in the back, legs and shoulders. Exercises 3, 22, 23, 24, 38, 41, 42 in Appendix A are among those recommended.

RUNNING

A walk speeded up becomes first a jog and then a run, but in the transformation certain characteristics of the locomotor pattern are altered. Major adjustments occur naturally, but people differ markedly in the degree to which they have refined their movements. Slow, heavy-footed, and ineffectual runners are all too common. They are seriously handicapped in many sports and, like awkward walkers, waste energy and offend the eye.

Why do so many women run poorly? The management of skirts and awareness of the aesthetic qualities of a narrow silhouette have long conditioned women to keep their knees close together. Although the habit may have been adopted without conscious intent, it persists and is recognized as a feminine characteristic. Thus, we see women trying to run by moving only from the knee down. Thighs and knees are barely separated while the lower leg kicks out behind at an angle.

There is no anatomical reason for women to run in this awkward manner. It may be comforting to know that there are sound reasons, however, for males to run *faster* than females. First of all, they enjoy a distinct anatomical advantage in their greater proportional leg length and slightly higher center of gravity. Running requires balance to be lost and regained speedily with every step. The male, being more unstable in structure and having a longer lever arm through which to apply force, is better suited to covering ground quickly. Force applied at a right angle to a surface is most effective. Here again, the masculine build is superior because it permits a more vertical push-off than can be achieved when legs are attached to the broader female pelvis.

These male advantages are small. Women runners in recent Olympic Games have broken men's speed records set in earlier years.

A check of the major technique points of running will help you avoid common errors. Most women *can* and *should* run better.

1. Body inclined forward from the ankles, degree increasing with speed.
2. Free leg swing from hips, movement line straight forward and backward.
3. Emphasis on knee lift forward without kickup behind.
4. Landing on ball of foot and toes in fast run, but on heel, then ball and toes in jog or slow run.
5. Forceful push-off with toes.
6. Abdominal muscles firm to stabilize trunk and mobilize force.
7. Springy ankle and foot action, light landing on feet.
8. Elbows bent at right angles, arms close to sides and swinging in opposition to legs.
9. Chin and chest high.

Training to run track events follows the procedures discussed under "Conditioning for Sports and Dance Participation," Chapter 9. You should keep in mind that sprints depend upon anerobic work capacity whereas middle and long distance running are aerobic events.

Conditioning to correct problems: menstrual, foot, back, tension

12

Women frequently are troubled by some uncomfortable ailments that stem in part from posture, exercise habits, physiological functions related to child-bearing, and even clothing. Principal among the problems are menstrual, foot and back pain, and excess tension. A brief discussion of causes, prevention, correction, and conditioning techniques is given in this chapter.

MENSTRUAL PROBLEMS

Menstruation is a physiological function occurring between puberty and meno-pause. Each month, every 28 days on the average, the uterus prepares itself for the possibility of conception by building up the blood supply and nu-tritive elements in the tissue of its walls in order to furnish for the ovum a suitable bed in which to develop.

The menstrual cycle can be thought of as starting when menstrual flow stops, for this is when the preparation for conception begins. In the first stage the maturation of the ovum is stimulated by a hormone secreted by the anterior lobe of the pituitary gland. The ovum then moves toward the surface of the ovary and enters the Graafian follicle. Meanwhile, the secre-tion of two female sex hormones causes the endometrium (the uterine lining) to thicken and to develop numerous small blood vessels. When fertilization does not occur, the endometrium and its small blood vessels break down and are eliminated by menstrual flow through the vagina. The average length of flow is 5 days.

Emotion, environmental conditions, and physiological state, among other factors, influence endocrine secretions. Thus, fluctuations in the usual cycle and differences in the flow may occur from period to period. Interestingly, the experience of going away to college is not infrequently the cause of tem-porary alterations in an individual's pattern. The menstrual process is, of course, an entirely normal one during which there should be no discomfort or, at most, minor sensations such as a feeling of congestion in the abdominal area or an awareness that body temperature is not regulated as efficiently as usual. Preceding and during the period there may be a weight gain and perhaps some swelling and tenderness of the breasts. These temporary conditions result from water retention caused by hormonal changes.

Beliefs about the advisability of exercise during the menstrual period have undergone profound change over the years. Where formerly women were counseled to rest as much as possible, they are now encouraged to continue normal activity. Seldom is there reason to curtail exercise or to avoid particular forms of exercise (12).

Good hygienic practices are essential during the period. Body odors form when the menstrual flow comes in contact with the air, and therefore frequent bathing and frequent changes of sanitary protection are important.

Young women sometimes question whether strenuous exercise adversely affects child-bearing. Research has refuted the misconceptions of earlier generations. Vigorous exercise habits are to be encouraged as they are beneficial rather than detrimental. (12)

If there is any discomfort during the menstrual period, the symptoms usually are some combination of uterine cramps, headache, nausea, backache, or leg ache, but probably no more than 20 to 30 percent of the cases of dysmenorrhea are attributable to organic causes. When the difficulty is at all severe, a physician's advice should be sought. If his findings are negative or if the problem is mild in the first place, there are steps that may alleviate the trouble. Your approach should be twofold: to make yourself more comfortable when there is pain and to prevent its reoccurrence by a conditioning program.

First Aid   First aid measures are position, heat, and exercise. Any position in which the hips are elevated facilitates the return of blood from the abdominal area to the heart and thus helps to relieve congestion. Even lying with a pillow under the hips may be of benefit. Two other recommended positions are as follows:

1. Kneel, hips high, forearms on the floor with the elbows just outside the knees. Turn the face to one side and rest the cheek on the floor.
2. Tip a straight chair without rungs forward so that the top of the back touches the floor. Place one bed pillow on the chair back and another over the underneath part of the seat. Kneel and lean forward to rest on the chair in a V position so that the thighs are against the chair back and the upper body is hanging over the back of the seat. This may seem a peculiar resting position but is actually very comfortable.

Abdominal exercise exerts a massaging action which also aids in reducing congestion in the pelvic area. You will be able to think of other variations of these exercises and probably will wish to choose equally mild movements. Several exercises listed in Appendix A which are good for this purpose are numbers 6, 7, 17, 21.

Attempts to relieve dysmenorrhea are at best palliative measures; prevention through conditioning is more to the point. When the problem is a functional one, poor abdominal muscle tone, fatigue, and tension may be contributing factors. Although relief is not guaranteed by exercises, it may well help.

According to Dr. Harvey Billig, dysmenorrhea is associated with lordosis, or swayback. Shortened, consequently tightened, ligamentous bands irritate peripheral nerves and cause pain in the pelvic area. The fascia can be stretched and the dysmenorrhea frequently eliminated or at least relieved by *conscientiously* practicing a preventive exercise between menstrual periods. So many women have found that this exercise really works that it is well worth the little time and effort it requires. (4) The Billig exercise is described and **shown on pages 72-73 of Appendix A.**

Anyone with functional dysmenorrhea should not only try the Billig exercise but should also do progressive resistance exercise for the abdominal muscles if there is any question as to their strength and firmness. This muscle group is important in preventing congestion in the pelvic area. You can devise a set of exercises appropriate in difficulty by referring to the sit-up series described in Chapter 5 or to the section on strengthening exercises in Chapter 4. Stair climbing, running, swimming, and all active sports and dance are helpful too.

FOOT PROBLEMS

Foot trouble, endured by 80 percent of adults, ranks next to back trouble in the list of orthopedic complaints of middle-aged Americans. It is sometimes hard during college years to imagine that any part of the body that now feels so comfortable and capable can let you down in the future. Parents and grandparents furnish evidence, however, that an ounce of prevention is advisable. Be good to your feet; they must last a lifetime.

Sources of Trouble   Problems with feet stem partly from the intricate anatomical design of the lower extremities, partly from choice of footwear, and partly from poor practices in using the feet.

The human foot is primarily a weight-bearing structure combining stability and flexibility. Approximately twenty-six bones are united by muscles, tendons, ligaments, and fascia to form two bridges which yield under the pressure of stepping and then spring back to position. Plainly seen is the longitudinal arch which runs from the heel along the inner border of the foot to the ball. The second bridge is the metatarsal arch, which runs across the ball of the foot from the great toe to the outer border.

A truly foot-shaped shoe is rare, and so-called space shoes which are molded to foot contours have not been accepted by the fashion world. Instead, as Cinderella's stepsisters did, we try to make our feet conform to whatever silhouette and heel height are currently popular. Of course, any shoe which modifies the position or action of the bare foot requires adaptation and may well result in friction or strain.

Kinds of Difficulties   While muscles are young, they are firm and resilient. Later strength and elasticity decrease and the effects of strain and malfunction become evident. Graphic, if not accurate, complaints are often heard about broken arches. What has happened is that the musculature no longer supports the bony arches adequately. The heads of the metatarsal bones may come in closer-than-normal contact with the floor at each step, thereby giving a sensation of walking on marbles. As the metatarsal, or transverse arch is depressed, the joints of the toes tend to rub on the shoes. Longitudinal arch trouble results in similar stresses.

The body reacts to protect itself against the pressure of the hard surfaces on which the weak foot walks and against the friction of the foot coverings. The joint of the great toe, and less frequently of the little toe, may enlarge to form bunions. Callouses may appear at stress points on the ball of the foot, the heel and the borders of the foot. Corns may form on or between the toes.

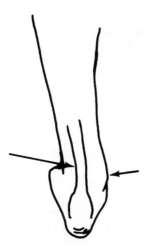

Fig. 8   Pronated Foot

Foot Mechanics   Two faults in using the feet properly are so common among the young as well as the old that they deserve special attention. Toeing out is conducive to *pronation*, in which the body weight is carried over the inner border of the foot. This is a weak position because downward force is exerted over the longitudinal arch where there is no supporting contact with the floor. The height of the arch is lowered by a pronated foot position and the inner ankle bones protrude; the heel cords deviate from a vertical line when viewed from the rear.

The second common error in foot mechanics is one of disuse. Many of us move about with little or no push-off with the toes. We simply rock forward on the sole of one shoe letting gravity pull us forward to the next step. Not only does this lessen the propulsive action of the foot in all forms of locomotion but it restricts the work performed by the toes. The muscles gradually lose strength and so contribute to an imbalance of forces in the foot structure.

Easing Fatigue and Foot Pain   The best preventive or corrective measures for feet that hurt are to select well-fitting shoes and hosiery, to strengthen the musculature of the feet, and to employ good foot mechanics. Supportive devices worn in the shoe are at best a crutch which, as a girdle does, may encourage even more muscle disuse and further deterioration.

Since every step is a foot exercise, it is important that foot position and action be checked for correct mechanics. Supplementary exercises over and above your daily walking also should be incorporated in the conditioning plan.

Exercise for the Metatarsal Arch   An erroneous but widespread belief is that toe curling, picking up objects with the toes, and walking on the outer borders of the feet are good strengtheners of the metatarsal arch. It is the longitudinal arch, primarily, that is exercised in such tasks. If you watch the foot in these actions you will see that the foot muscles are contracted along the length of the sole. Since the transverse arch runs across the foot, it is exercised by movement that contracts horizontal muscles. Few exercises isolate this movement but one that does follows:

Metatarsal Lift (strengthening).   Sit barefooted with sole of foot on floor. Hold toes flat with the fingers. Now try to elevate the ball of the foot so that the tendons stand out down the instep. The heel must remain on the floor and the toes must not curl at all. With practice, the transverse arch will assume a domelike curve and, in time, the exercise can be done without the aid of the hands. See below.

Exercise for the Longitudinal Arch   The key element in strengthening the long arch is to do movements in which the inner borders of the feet are lifted. A series of exercises for this purpose is given in Appendix A, number 14. You can easily devise other similar exercises.

Exercises for the Achilles Tendon   When high heels are popular, the Achilles Tendon sometimes becomes shortened so that the range of ankle motion is limited. Exercises in which the feet are slowly brought toward the shins to stretch the tendons are helpful. Numbers 28 and 31 are recommended.

BACK TROUBLE

Back pain has become so commonplace in the United States that it incapacitates thousands each year. The lower back, the lumbo-sacral area, is most often the site of the difficulty. The causes of pain and fatigue are legion, and medical sleuthing may be necessary for an accurate diagnosis. Predisposing factors are weak abdominal muscles and the inability of the lower back to withstand a great amount of force.

Weight lifting is a very low risk activity if safety precautions are followed. How should you lift a barbell from the floor to avoid injury to the back?

The high incidence of injuries to the back from the use of poor biomechanics in lifting is hardly surprising when one understands that merely straightening up from a forward-bend position centers a force of a quarter of a ton in the lower back! If an object is lifted from the floor by bending forward with the knees straight, the length of the lever arm from the axis at the lumbo-sacral spine to the shoulders has the effect of multiplying the weight of the object twelve to sixteen times. To lift heavy objects with the back rather than with the leg muscles, particularly if the back is twisted to the side as you lift, always invites back injury.

The abdominal muscles play an important role in stabilizing the trunk during large movements. When the vertical and diagonal abdominal musculature is strong, it provides a firm, relatively motionless center which acts as a brace for motion in peripheral body parts. Lax abdominal muscles, on the contrary, permit the body to slip into a swayback position that is subject to strain.

Anyone with back problems should seek medical advice to determine whether the difficulties are functional. If so, a three-part conditioning program is in order. Step 1 is to correct faulty postural alignment, paying special attention to reducing an exaggerated curve in the lumbar spine. Step 2 is to study the proper biomechanics of lifting, carrying, pushing, pulling, and other movements in which the body moves against a resisting force (Chapter 3). Step 3 is to improve the strength of the abdominal and lower back muscles.

There is a misconception that muscles in the lumbar area should be stretched but not strengthened because of their tendency to be shortened in most cases of poor standing posture. Every muscle in the body is designed to be used. All should be strong as well as flexible. Sample exercises listed in Appendix A that may help problem backs include numbers 2, 3, 6, 12, 16, 17, 21, 45.

RELAXATION

The pitch and tempo of modern living seem steadily to increase. The intellect accepts the situation, but the physical and emotional being often responds to the bombardment of stimuli with less aplomb. Many more or less disabling complaints can be attributed in part to the complexities and disturbances of our way of life.

Causes of Tension   Not only is man affected by external impact on the senses but by his own emotional makeup. Environmentally and internally induced tensions are mutually augmentative. Each individual has his own tension threshold above which stress makes itself felt. Each also has his own predisposition toward certain expressions of tension. One reacts with a headache, another with a stiff neck, a third is subject to digestive upsets. The cause of tension may be identical, but the effect may be insomnia, nervous fatigue, muscle spasms, hypertension, high blood pressure, and the like.

From Tension to Relaxation   Half the battle in combating tension is learning to pace oneself so that there is rhythm and balance in the pattern of work and play, haste and leisurely action. The development of a long-range outlook should be nurtured in order to keep small irritations and troubles in proper perspective. If something is not going to matter a year or five years from now, such recognition makes a problem dwindle in importance.

One specific antidote for excess tension is physical activity to the point of fatigue, for the "fight or flight" instinct remains strong in all of us. Either action suffices to relieve tension; what cannot be borne with equanimity is restraint. The vigorous sports in which there is all-out effort, marshalling of forces and exertion of power are great stabilizers and reducers of undesirable tension. In fact, one of the most enjoyable products of exercise is the comfortable feeling of muscular quiet that ensues.

Whereas demanding physical exertion is helpful in releasing emotional and physiological tensions, conditioning oneself to conserve energy is equally beneficial. Energy used in tightening muscles that are unnecessary to a task is energy wasted. Early fatigue and inept performance result.

Sleep in adequate amounts is as essential as exercise in preventing or overcoming excess tension. Not everyone requires the same number of hours or is habituated to the same pattern of sleep and wakefulness, yet everyone must yield to the physiological need for rest. Ironically, if the urge to sleep is too long denied, chronic fatigue may make the sleeping state more difficult to attain.

It should not be thought that all tension is bad or is a result of stress. Tonicity, a small amount of contraction, is a normal and necessary state in all muscles. Tension, whether mental or physical, is as essential to accomplishment as is relaxation. What is bad is an improper balance or an incorrect timing of contraction and relaxation. The degree of tension above the natural tonicity of muscle tissue and the alternation of contraction and release should be brought under conscious control. The individual who has learned to do this is able to move effectively, smoothly, forcefully, and with a minimum of effort. He is also able to remain at rest without a high residual level of muscular contraction.

The art of conscious relaxation can be learned. Yoga is one of several approaches and the Jacobson technique is another. The latter system stresses kinesthetic awareness of muscle contraction and release.

Whatever conscious relaxation system you use, first try to identify the circumstances in your own life which produce tension symptoms. If these causes can be eliminated or modified, improvement is assured. The next step is to heighten the ability to recognize excess tension. Strangely, we often believe that we are relaxed when an undue amount of contraction exists. One quick check of your perception of tension will give you an idea of your present level of conscious control. Lie on your back with arms relaxed at sides. A partner lifts your non-wristwatch forearm, then unexpectedly lets go. If your forearm remains in the air or descends slowly you are *not* relaxed. The arm should drop limply, a dead weight.

The alternation of strong contraction and sudden release of tension is the basis of training for conscious relaxation in the Jacobson system (18). A sample conditioning program based on that method appears in Appendix A, number 20, and should be helpful in overcoming tension problems as will exercises numbers 8, 18, 19, 35.

Bibliography and recommended readings

References starred are recommended as supplementary readings.

*1. ALLSEN, PHILIP E.; HARRISON, JOYCE M.; and VANCE, BARBARA. *Fitness for Life.* Dubuque, Iowa: Wm. C. Brown Company Publishers, 1976.

2. ASTRAND, PER-OLOF. "Physiological Condition and Its Assessment" in *Exercise and the Heart,* edited by Robert L. Morse, pp. 46-47. Springfield, Ill.: Charles C Thomas, Publisher, 1972.

3. BERGER, RICHARD A. Effect of Varied Weight Training Programs on Strength. *Research Quarterly of the AAHPER* 33:168-181, 1962.

4. BILLIG, HARVEY E., JR. and LOWENDAHL, EVELYN. *Mobilization of the Human Body.* Stanford, Calif.: Stanford University Press, 1949.

*5. BOWERMAN, WILLIAM and HARRIS, W. E. *Jogging.* New York: Grosset & Dunlap, Inc., 1967.

*6. BROER, MARION R. *Efficiency of Human Movement.* Philadelphia: W. B. Saunders Company, 1966.

*7. COOPER, KENNETH H. *The New Aerobics.* New York: M. Evans and Company, Inc., 1970.

*8. COOPER, MILDRED and COOPER, KENNETH H. *Aerobics for Women.* New York: M. Evans and Company, Inc., 1972.

*9. CURETON, THOMAS C. "Run for Your Life." in *The Healthy Life,* p. 38. New York: Time, Inc., 1966.

*10. DEVRIES, HERBERT A. *Physiology of Exercise.* 2d ed. Dubuque, Iowa: Wm. C. Brown Company Publishers, 1974.

11. EKBLOM, B. et al. Effect of Training on Circulatory Response to Exercise. *Journal of Applied Physiology* 24:518-528, 1968.

12. ERDELYI, G. J. Gynecological Survey of Female Athletes. *Journal of Sports Medicine* 2:174-179, 1962.

*13. FEFFER, H. All About Backache. *Reader's Digest,* p. 203, December 1971.

14. FOX, SAMUEL M. and BOYER, J. L. "Physical Activity and Coronary Heart Disease," in *Physical Fitness Research Digest,* edited by H. H. Clarke, Washington, D. C.: President's Council on Physical Fitness and Sports, Series 2, No. 2, 1972.

*15. HOCKEY, ROBERT V. *Physical Fitness.* 2d ed. St. Louis: The C. V. Mosby Company, 1973.

16. HOLLAND, GEORGE J. The Physiology of Flexibility: A Review. *Kinesiology Review*. pp. 49-62, 1968.
*17. HOLLAND, GEORGE J. and DAVIS, ELWOOD C. *Values of Physical Activity.* 3d ed. Dubuque, Iowa: Wm. C. Brown Company Publishers, 1975.
*18. JACOBSON, EDMUND. *You Must Relax.* New York: McGraw-Hill Book Company, 1962.
*19. JOHNSON, BARRY L. and NELSON, JACK K. *Practical Measurements for Evaluation in Physical Education.* Minneapolis: Burgess Pub. Co., 1974.
20. KARVONEN, M. J. "Effects of Vigorous Exercise on the Heart," in *Work and the Heart*, edited by F. F. Rosenbaum and E. Belknap. New York: Paul B. Hoeber, Inc., 1959.
21. LOGAN, GENE A. *Differential Applications of Resistance and Resulting Strength Measured at Varying Degrees of Knee Flexion.* Unpublished doctoral dissertation, University of Southern California, Los Angeles, 1960.
22. LOGAN, GENE A. and EGSTRON, GLEN H. The Effects of Slow and Fast Stretching on the Sacrofemoral Angle. *Journal of the Association for Physical and Mental Rehabilitation* 15:85-89, 1961.
23. LOGAN, GENE A. and FOREMAN, KENNETH E. Strength-Endurance Continuum. *The Physical Educator* 18:103, 1961.
24. MASSEY, BENJAMIN H. and CLAUDEL, NORMAN L. Effect of Systematic Heavy Resistance Exercise on Range of Joint Movement in Young Adults. *Research Quarterly of the AAHPER* 27:41-51, 1956.
*25. MASSEY, BENJAMIN et al. *The Kinesiology of Weight Lifting.* Dubuque, Iowa: Wm. C. Brown Company Publishers, 1959.
*26. MAYER, JEAN. *Overweight: Causes, Cost, and Control.* Englewood Cliffs, N. J.: Prentice-Hall, Inc., 1968.
27. POLLOCK, MICHAEL L.; CURETON, THOMAS K.; and GRENINGER, L. Effects of Frequency of Training on Working Capacity, Cardiovascular Function, and Body Composition of Adult Men. *Medicine and Science in Sports* 1:70-74, 1969.
*28. President's Council on Physical Fitness. N.d. *Adult Physical Fitness.* Washington, D. C.: U.S. Government Printing Office.
29. ROWELL, LORING B. "Human Cardiovascular Responses to Exercise," in *Exercise and the Heart*, edited by Robert L. Morse, pp. 5-26. Springfield, Ill.: Charles C Thomas Publisher, 1972.
*30. Royal Canadian Air Force. *Exercise Plans for Physical Fitness.* Rev. U.S. ed. Ottawa: Pocket Books, Inc., 1962.
31. SCHERER, PAUL R. A Clinical Study to Determine the Effects of Wearing Earth Shoes. *Journal of the American Podiatry Association* 65: 422-443, May 1975.
32. SCOTT, M. GLADYS and FRENCH, ESTHER. *Measurement and Evaluation in Physical Education.* Dubuque, Iowa: Wm. C. Brown Company Publishers, 1959.
*33. SORANI, ROBERT P. *Circuit Training.* Dubuque, Iowa: Wm. C. Brown Company Publishers, 1966.
*34. U.S. DEPARTMENT OF AGRICULTURE. *Food and Your Weight.* Home and Garden Bulletin No. 74. Washington, D. C.: Government Printing Office, 1960.
*35. WITTEN, CHET. Cardiovascular Step Test for College Females. *Research Quarterly of the AAHPER* 44:46-50, 1973.
36. YESSIS, MICHAEL. *Relationships Between Varying Combinations of Resistances and Repetitions in the Strength-Endurance Continuum.* Unpublished doctoral dissertation, University of Southern California, Los Angeles, 1963.

Appendix A: Representative exercises

The first thirty-five isotonic and isometric exercises that follow are representative of movement patterns designed to strengthen, stretch, relax or develop endurance. Some of the exercises also are particularly good for warming up or tapering off. Whatever the movements, by analyzing each exercise you can pick out the key actions that make it effective for its main purpose. You can then recombine or separate these essential actions as well as modify or intensify the work load, and thus devise countless variations of your own. The number of repetitions, cadence, or length of time to be devoted to an exercise depends on your purposes, present level of condition, and the total content of your conditioning program.

Exercises numbered 36-47 are a weight training series. The number of executions suggested for each is for a beginner starting a strength development program.

1. *Arm Swings*. Stand, feet about 12 inches apart. Swing both arms up and forward to shoulder height, then back down and out to sides to shoulder height. Continue swings rhythmically. (warm-up and relaxing shoulder girdle)
2. *Back Fly*. Lie on your face, arms outstretched at shoulder height. With chin tucked in, stretch from head to toes, lifting head, arms and feet no more than 6 inches. (strengthening back muscles and stretching front of shoulders)

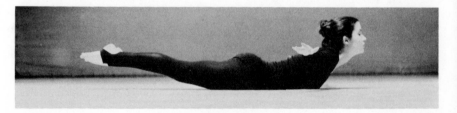

Fig. 9   Back Fly

3. *Back Leg Lift.* Lie prone, legs spread about 15 inches, toes down, palms on floor by shoulders in push-up position. Lift one straight leg about 12 inches above floor, stretching out with toes. Repeat with other leg. (strengthening neck, back and hip)

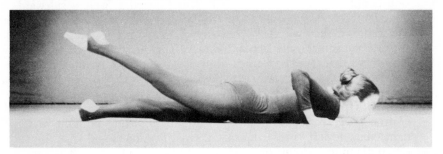

Fig. 10 Back Leg Lift

4. *Ball Throw.* Repeatedly throw a ball against a wall as hard and as rapidly as possible. Then repeatedly toss the ball upward as high and as fast as possible. (strengthening throwing arm and shoulder)
5. *Billig Exercise.* Stand, feet together, knees locked, the right side 18 inches from a wall, the right forearm placed horizontally against the wall at

a   b

Fig. 11a, b   Billig Exercise

shoulder height. Place the left hand against the hollow at the left hip joint so that the heel of the hand is high and well back, the fingers slanting down and forward. Tuck the pelvis and push with the heel of the left hand to move the hips diagonally forward toward the wall. The motion is not directly toward the wall, it is *forward* as well as sideward. If done correctly, few people can move far enough to make the hips touch the wall, but they will feel a real stretch in the pelvic area. This simple exercise consumes only a few moments, but if it is to be effective it is essential that it be performed faithfully three times on each side, three times per day, every day except during the menstrual period for at least two or three months. (prevention of dysmenorrhea)

6. *Curl Sit-Ups.* Hook-lying position, finger tips touching back of head. Flatten lower back, lift head and curl up to sitting position to touch right elbow to left knee. Continue alternating elbows and knees touched. (strengthening abdominals)

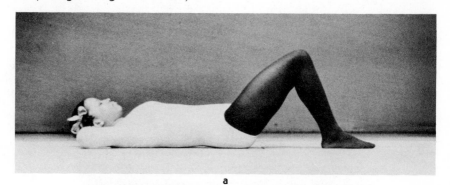

a

b

Fig. 12a, b   Curl Sit-Ups

7. *Head and Neck Lift.* Back-lying position. Lift head and neck, hold 5 counts, then lower. (strengthening abdominals)
8. *Hip Lift.* Lie on your back with knees bent and arms at the sides, palms down. While you count to twenty very slowly, gradually elevate the hips. Do not hold your breath. The body is supported on feet, arms and shoulders. Take twenty counts to return to starting position. This exercise combines the influence of gravity and massage in facilitating the return of venous blood to the heart thus slowing its rate. (relaxation)

Fig. 13   Hip Lift

9. *Inverted V.* Lie on your back. Draw knees to chest and then straighten legs toward the ceiling. Grasp outside of thighs and resist movement as you slowly separate legs sideward as far as possible. Grasp inside of thighs

Fig. 14a   Inverted V

Fig. 14b   Inverted V

and resist as you slowly return legs to closed position. (stretching and strengthening legs)

10. *Jumping Jill.* From a normal stand, jump to a side stride, clapping hands overhead. Jump again, bring feet back together and hands to sides. (warm-up or endurance)

11. *Knee Push-Ups.* Lie prone, palms of hands on floor by shoulders, legs together and lower legs raised toward ceiling. Keeping chin tucked in and body straight from head to knee, push with arms and shoulders until elbows are straight and weight rests on hands and knees. Bend elbows to touch chin or chest only to floor. (strengthening arms, shoulders and abdominals)

a

b

Fig. 15a, b   Knee Push-Ups

12. *Knees Over.* Lie on your back, arms to sides at shoulder height, and draw
    knees to chest. Keeping shoulders flat and knees together, let bent legs
    fall to one side. When knees touch floor, bring legs back to chest and
    repeat to other side. (trunk flexibility)

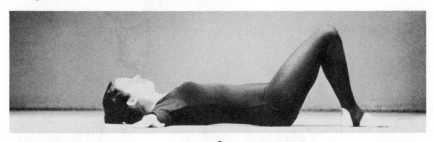

a

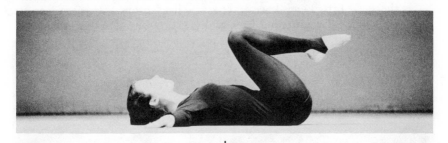

b

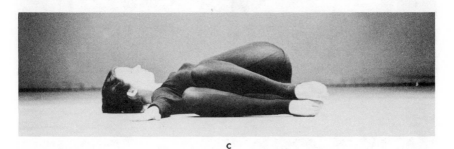

c

Fig. 16a, b, c   Knees Over

13. *Leg Swings.* Stand on left foot, arms lifted for balance. Swing right leg
    forward and backward, keeping knee straight. Do four low swings, then
    four high. Change legs. (warm-up and relaxing legs and hips)
14. *Longitudinal Arch Series* (strengthening)
    a. While seated with bare feet on the nearer end of a towel, gather up
       the material by alternately grasping it with the toes of each foot.
    b. Sit on floor, legs in front, knees straight. With both feet moving si-
       multaneously, describe small circles. Start by flexing the feet toward
       you, then outward and on around, pulling hard as the soles turn toward
       each other.
    c. Use the toes to pick up marbles, one at a time, and to replace them
       on the floor.

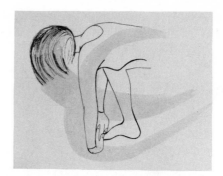

Fig. 17   Metatarsal Lift

15. *Metatarsal Lift* (strengthening). See page 64 for description.
16. *Out and In.* Start on hands and knees. Stretch one leg backward and high as the head lifts. Draw knee to chest as head drops. Alternate legs after eight times. (strengthening back and legs)

a

b

Fig. 18a, b   Out and In

17. *Pumping.* Lie on back, knees bent. Contract abdominal muscles to flatten lower back against the floor. Relax abdominals and arch lower back. Movements should be alternated slowly and rhythmically. (dysmenorrhea and strengthening abdominals)
18. *Rag Doll.* Sit tailor fashion with spine and shoulders erect. Drop head back as far as possible and slowly circle it to the left, front, right, and back. After four circles, change direction. (stretching neck and shoulders and relaxation)

Fig. 19   Rag Doll

19. *Reach and Fall.* Stand, feet apart. Slowly stretch the left hand high. Let arm fall. Repeat with right arm, then both arms. As the two arms fall, let the trunk and head drop forward. Hold a few seconds. Return to starting position. (relaxation and tapering off)
20. *Relaxation Series*
    a. Lie on your back, eyes closed. Contract the gluteal muscles as forcefully as possible. Hold for several seconds and then let go suddenly. Repeat several times at a leisurely pace. Alternately tighten and relax other muscle groups until you have included gluteals, abdomen, each leg separately and both together, each arm separately and both together, one arm and leg in combination, both arms and both legs together, whole body.
    b. On your back, draw one shoulder up to the ear, hold and then drop it suddenly. After a few repetitions use the other shoulder and finally shrug both simultaneously.
    c. Make faces, the more grotesque the grimaces the better. After holding the contorted positions a few seconds, let go so completely that even your jaw drops.
    d. Lie on your back. Without preliminary tensing of muscles consciously try to make one foot and ankle entirely limp, then the other. When they feel relaxed and heavy, direct your attention to another muscle group. Continue until you have focused your efforts on all body parts. Then mentally recheck each part and if tension has developed, try to release it.

Stretching exercises performed slowly and rhythmically comprise the last part of the relaxation conditioning program.

21. *Rocking Chair.* Lie on your back with knees drawn to chest and arms wrapped around lower legs to hold them close to body. Rock forward and backward trying to come to a sitting position. (strengthening abdominals and stretching lower back)

Fig. 20 Rocking Chair

22. *Rope Skipping.* Using an individual rope, jump lightly and continuously. (warm-up or endurance)
23. *Run and Skip.* Lifting knees to bring feet at least 4 inches from floor, run lightly in place sixteen times. (Count one each time left foot steps.) Do four skips forward and four backward. Repeat skips. (strengthening feet and legs or endurance)
24. *Run in Place.* Lifting knees to bring feet at least 4 inches from floor, run in place. (strengthening feet and legs or endurance)
25. *Ski Stretch.* From a stand, feet together and arms stretched overhead, drop slowly forward from the hips until the palms or fingers are on the

Fig. 21 Ski Stretch

floor and the head hangs limp between the arms. Hold. Now raise arms, head and trunk until you are in a right-angle position, back and arms parallel with floor. Lift head and hold. (stretching hamstrings and strengthening back and neck)

26. *Sprinter's Start.* Crouch with palms on floor below shoulders, arms straight, one knee bent, and other leg extended behind. Bounce hips down and up two times, then take weight on hands to change lead leg. Repeat bounces and change. (agility, strengthening shoulder girdle, abdomen, legs and hips)

Fig. 22   Sprinter's Start

27. *Squat Thrust Jump.* (1) From a stand, squat to place palms flat on floor; (2) with weight supported on hands, thrust legs backward; (3) thrust feet apart; (4) feet back together; (5) back to squat position; (6) return to stand. (strengthening arms, shoulders, abdomen, hips and legs; agility and endurance)

a   b

Fig. 23a, b   Squat Thrust Jump

c

Fig. 23c   Squat Thrust Jump

28. *Tendon Stretch.* Stand with balls of feet on a block of wood, a stair tread, or a thick book. Slowly dip the heels as far as possible and then rise on tiptoes. (ankle flexibility)

29. *Thigh Trimmer.* Lie on your side, bracing with one palm on the floor in front and the underneath arm overhead. Lift leg sideways toward ceiling and then return to place. Alternate sides after 1/2 the total number of lifts. (strengthening and stretching legs)

Fig. 24   Thigh Trimmer

30. *Toe Touch.* From a stand, bend forward slowly to bring hands to floor. Hold, then return to stand. (stretching hamstrings and lower back and strengthening back)

31. *Toes Up.* Sit on the floor, legs in front, knees straight. Alternately flex and extend the ankles as far as possible. (ankle flexibility)

32. *V-Sit.* Lie on your back, arms at sides. Jackknife to touch fingers to ankles, hold 5 counts then return to starting position. Keep head and back in straight alignment and knees extended throughout.

33. *Wall Sit.* Assume a sitting position with head, shoulders and hips braced

Fig. 25   V-Sit

firmly against a wall and thighs parallel with floor. Maintain position
as long as possible. (strengthening legs)
34. *Waltz Time Swing.* Stand with feet apart and arms extended high to
one side. Bend knees and hips and let head hang while swinging arms
in an arc, down and across in front of body and up to opposite side. After
one swing in each direction, make a full circle. Relax neck and shoulders
on every downward swing. (relaxation and tapering off)

a   b   c
Fig. 26a, b, c   Waltz Time Swing

35. *Wing Spread.* Sitting, bring arms forward and up to shoulder level. Slowly stretch arms backward as far as you can while tilting chin up. Hold. Return to starting position. (stretching neck and shoulders and relaxation)

a   b

Fig. 27a, b   Wing Spread

WEIGHT TRAINING STRENGTH EXERCISES

36. *Chest Press.* Six executions. Kneel on one knee and other foot, grasp bar of variable resistance machine and pull to chest with elbows out, then slowly extend arms. (arm flexors and upper back)

Fig. 28   Chest Press

37. *Hand Gripping.* Six executions in each direction and in each hand position. Sit on a bench holding barbell across the knees in a palms up position with forearms resting on thighs. Alternately flex and extend the wrists. Perform same actions holding bar in a palms down position. (wrist flexors and extensors)

Fig. 29   Hand Gripping

38. *Heel Lift.* Six executions. Stand holding barbell in neck rest position with a palms down grip. Rise to the balls of the feet, then bring heels down. (feet, ankles and lower legs)
39. *High Pull-Up.* Six executions. Stand holding the center of a barbell against the thighs, hands together in a palms down grip. Lift the bar to shoulder height, elbows leading, then lower it to starting position. (arm and shoulder flexors)
40. *Knee Lift.* One execution. Hang from a horizontal bar. Lift and lower the knees. (abdominals and hip flexors)
41. *Leg Press.* Six executions. Sit with knees bent and feet against lower pedals of variable resistance machine. Push to straighten knees, then slowly return to starting position. (knee extensors)
42. *Posterior Leg Lift.* Six executions. Stand on a low bench with a weight attached to the sole of one foot. Place one hand on the wall or hold a support for balance. Alternately flex and straighten the knee. (knee flexors)

Fig. 30   Heel Lift

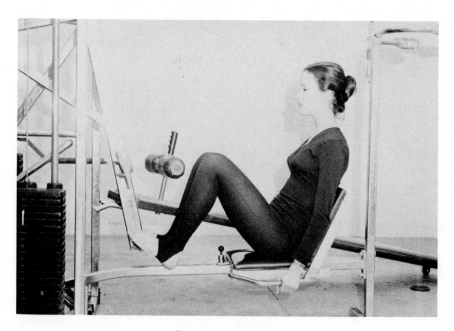

Fig. 31   Leg Press

43. *Side Bend.* Six executions each side. Stand holding a dumbbell in each hand at shoulder height, elbows close to sides. Alternately bend from one side to the other. (lateral trunk flexors)
44. *Sitting Overhead Press.* Six executions. Start seated on bench holding barbell in chest rest position with palms down. Push bar overhead to arm's length, then lower slowly. (arm and shoulder extensors)

a   b

Fig. 32a, b   Sitting Overhead Press

45. *Sit-Ups.* Six executions. Lie supine, knees bent, feet hooked under a barbell, and a weight plate held behind head. Alternately curl halfway to sitting position, then uncurl to floor. (abdominals)
46. *Two Arm Curls.* Six executions. Stand with back against a wall holding barbell in front of thighs with a palms up grip. Raise bar to shoulder height, keeping elbows straight, then lower slowly. (arm flexors)
47. *Weighted Leg Lift.* Six executions each side. Lie on your side, supporting arm overhead and supporting leg bent at hip and knee. Lift and lower the top leg with ankle weight attached. (lateral hip flexors)

Appendix B: Heights and weights of women[1]

The table is based on average rather than ideal figures. You probably will wish to consider the weight given as near maximum. For ages 17, 18, and 19 years, subtract one pound for each year under age 20. For example: height— 5'4", average frame, age 18 years. 122 pounds on table minus 2 for age = 120 pounds maximum desirable weight.

Height (without shoes)	Weight (without clothing) (pounds)		
	Small Frame	Average Frame	Large Frame
5 feet	100	109	118
5 feet 1 inch	104	112	121
5 feet 2 inches	107	115	125
5 feet 3 inches	110	118	128
5 feet 4 inches	113	122	132
5 feet 5 inches	116	125	135
5 feet 6 inches	120	129	139
5 feet 7 inches	123	132	142
5 feet 8 inches	126	136	146
5 feet 9 inches	130	140	151
5 feet 10 inches	133	144	156
5 feet 11 inches	137	148	161
6 feet	141	152	166

[1]Tabled heights and weights taken from Food and Your Weight. Home and Garden Bulletin No. 74, U.S. Dept. of Agriculture. Washington, D. C.: U.S. Government Printing Office, revised edition, 1967.

Appendix C: Calorie expenditure per minute for various activities[1]

Count only time of actual activity	90	99	108	117	125	134	143	152	161	170	178	187	196	205	213	222	231
Archery	3.1	3.4	3.7	4.0	4.5	4.6	4.9	5.2	5.5	5.8	6.1	6.4	6.7	7.0	7.3	7.6	7.9
Badminton (recreation)	3.4	3.8	4.1	4.4	4.8	5.1	5.4	5.6	6.1	6.4	6.8	7.1	7.4	7.8	8.1	8.3	8.8
Badminton (competition)	5.9	6.4	7.0	7.6	8.1	8.7	9.3	9.9	10.4	11.0	11.6	12.1	12.7	13.3	13.9	14.4	15.0
Baseball (player)	2.8	3.1	3.4	3.6	3.9	4.2	4.5	4.7	5.0	5.3	5.5	5.8	6.1	6.4	6.6	6.9	7.2
Baseball (pitcher)	3.5	3.9	4.3	4.6	5.0	5.3	5.7	6.0	6.4	6.7	7.1	7.4	7.8	8.1	8.5	8.8	9.2
Basketball (half-court)	2.5	3.3	3.5	3.8	4.1	4.4	4.7	4.9	5.3	5.6	5.9	6.2	6.4	6.7	7.0	7.3	7.5
Basketball (moderate)	4.2	4.6	5.0	5.5	5.9	6.3	6.7	7.1	7.5	7.9	8.3	8.8	9.2	9.6	10.0	10.4	10.8
Basketball (competition)	5.9	6.5	7.1	7.7	8.2	8.8	9.4	10.0	10.6	11.1	11.7	12.3	12.9	13.5	14.0	14.6	15.0
Bicycling (level) 5.5 mph	3.0	3.3	3.6	3.9	4.2	4.5	4.8	5.1	5.4	5.6	5.9	6.2	6.5	6.8	7.1	7.4	7.7
Bicycling (level) 13 mph	6.4	7.1	7.7	8.3	8.9	9.6	10.2	10.8	11.4	12.1	12.7	13.4	14.0	14.6	15.2	15.9	16.5
Bowling (nonstop)	4.0	4.4	4.8	5.2	5.6	5.9	6.3	6.7	7.1	7.5	7.9	8.3	8.7	9.1	9.5	9.8	10.2
Calisthenics	3.0	3.3	3.6	3.9	4.2	4.5	4.8	5.1	5.4	5.6	5.9	6.2	6.5	6.8	7.1	7.4	7.7
Canoeing 2.5 mph	1.8	1.9	2.0	2.2	2.3	2.5	2.7	3.0	3.2	3.4	3.6	3.7	3.9	4.1	4.7	4.4	4.6
Canoeing 4.0 mph	4.2	4.6	5.0	5.5	5.9	6.3	6.7	7.1	7.5	7.9	8.3	8.7	9.2	9.4	10.0	10.5	10.8

BODY WEIGHT

[1]Adapted from *Fitness for Life*, 1976, by Allsen, Philip; Harrison, Joyce; and Vance, Barbara. Reprinted by courtesy of Wm. C. Brown Company Publishers.

Appendix C —Calorie Expenditure Per Minute for Various Activities (Continued) ....

Count only time of actual activity	BODY WEIGHT																
	90	99	108	117	125	134	143	152	161	170	178	187	196	205	213	222	231
Dance, Modern (moderate)	2.5	2.8	3.0	3.2	3.5	3.7	4.0	4.2	4.5	4.7	5.0	5.2	5.4	5.7	5.9	6.2	6.4
Dance, Modern (vigorous)	3.4	3.7	4.1	4.4	4.7	5.1	5.4	5.7	6.1	6.4	6.7	7.1	7.4	7.7	8.1	8.4	8.7
Dance, Foxtrot	2.7	2.9	3.2	3.4	3.7	4.0	4.2	4.5	4.7	5.0	5.3	5.5	5.8	6.0	6.3	6.6	6.8
Dance, Rumba	4.2	4.6	5.0	5.4	5.8	6.2	6.6	7.0	7.4	7.8	8.2	8.6	9.0	9.4	9.8	10.2	10.6
Dance, Square	4.1	4.5	4.9	5.3	5.7	6.1	6.5	6.9	7.3	7.8	8.1	8.5	8.9	9.3	9.7	10.1	10.5
Dance, Waltz	3.1	3.4	3.7	4.0	4.3	4.6	4.9	5.2	5.5	5.8	6.1	6.4	6.7	7.0	7.3	7.6	7.9
Fencing (moderate)	3.0	3.3	3.6	3.9	4.2	4.5	4.8	5.1	5.4	5.6	6.0	6.2	6.5	6.8	7.1	7.4	7.7
Fencing (vigorous)	6.2	6.8	7.4	8.0	8.6	9.2	9.8	8.7	11.0	11.6	12.2	12.8	13.4	14.0	14.6	15.2	15.8
Golf (twosome)	3.3	3.6	3.9	4.2	4.5	4.8	5.2	5.5	5.8	6.1	6.4	6.7	7.1	7.4	7.7	8.0	8.3
Golf (foursome)	2.4	2.7	2.9	3.2	3.4	3.6	3.9	4.1	4.3	4.6	4.8	5.1	5.3	5.5	5.8	6.0	6.2
Hiking, 40 lb. pack (3.0 mph)	4.1	4.5	4.9	5.3	5.7	6.1	6.5	6.9	7.3	7.7	8.1	8.5	8.9	9.3	9.7	10.1	10.5
Horseback Riding (walk)	2.0	2.3	2.4	2.6	2.8	3.0	3.1	3.3	3.5	3.7	3.9	4.1	4.3	4.5	4.7	4.9	5.1
Horseback Riding (trot)	4.1	4.4	4.8	5.2	5.6	6.0	6.4	6.8	7.2	7.6	8.0	8.4	8.8	9.2	9.6	10.0	10.4
Horseshoe Pitching	2.1	2.3	2.5	2.7	3.0	3.3	3.4	3.6	3.8	4.0	4.2	4.4	4.6	4.8	5.0	5.2	5.4
Judo, Karate	7.7	8.5	9.2	10.0	10.7	11.5	12.2	13.0	13.7	14.5	15.2	16.0	16.7	17.5	18.2	19.0	19.7
Mountain Climbing	6.0	6.5	7.2	7.8	8.4	9.0	9.6	10.1	10.7	11.3	11.9	12.5	13.1	13.7	14.3	14.8	15.4

Appendix C —Calorie Expenditure Per Minute for Various Activities (Continued) ....

Count only time of actual activity	BODY WEIGHT																
	90	99	108	117	125	134	143	152	161	170	178	187	196	205	213	222	231
Paddleball—Racquetball	5.9	6.4	7.0	7.6	8.1	8.7	9.3	9.9	10.4	11.0	11.6	12.1	12.7	13.3	13.9	14.4	15.0
Pool—Billiards	1.1	1.2	1.3	1.4	1.5	1.6	1.7	1.8	1.9	2.0	2.1	2.2	2.4	2.5	2.6	2.7	2.8
Rowing (recreation)	3.0	3.3	3.6	3.9	4.2	4.5	4.8	5.1	5.4	5.6	6.0	6.2	6.5	6.8	7.1	7.5	7.7
Rowing (machine)	8.2	9.0	9.8	10.6	11.4	12.2	13.0	13.8	14.6	15.4	16.2	17.0	17.8	18.6	19.4	20.2	21.0
Running, 11 min. mile 5.5 mph	6.4	7.1	7.7	8.3	9.0	9.6	10.2	10.8	11.5	12.1	12.7	13.4	14.0	14.6	15.2	15.9	16.5
Running, 8.5 min. mile 7 mph	8.4	9.2	10.0	10.8	11.7	12.5	13.3	14.1	14.9	15.7	16.6	17.4	18.2	19.0	19.8	20.7	21.5
Running, 7 min. mile 9 mph	9.3	10.2	11.1	12.9	13.1	13.9	14.8	15.7	16.6	17.5	18.9	19.3	20.2	21.1	22.1	23.0	23.9
Running, 5 min. mile 12 mph	11.8	13.0	14.1	15.3	16.4	17.6	18.7	19.9	21.0	22.2	23.3	24.5	25.6	26.8	27.9	29.1	30.2
Stationary Running 140 counts/min.	14.6	16.1	17.5	18.9	20.4	21.8	23.2	24.6	26.1	27.5	28.9	30.4	31.8	33.2	34.6	36.1	37.5
Sprinting	13.8	15.2	16.6	17.9	19.2	20.5	21.9	23.3	24.7	26.1	27.3	28.7	30.0	31.4	32.7	34.0	35.4
Sailing	1.8	2.0	2.1	2.3	2.4	2.7	2.8	3.0	3.2	3.4	3.6	3.8	3.9	4.1	4.3	4.4	4.6
Skating (moderate)	3.4	3.8	4.1	4.4	4.8	5.1	5.4	5.8	6.1	6.4	6.8	7.1	7.4	7.8	8.1	8.3	8.8
Skating (vigorous)	6.2	6.8	7.4	8.0	8.6	9.2	9.8	9.9	11.0	11.6	12.2	12.8	13.4	14.0	14.6	15.2	15.8
Skiing (downhill)	5.8	6.4	6.9	7.5	8.1	8.6	9.2	9.8	10.3	10.9	11.4	12.0	12.6	13.1	13.7	14.3	14.8
Skiing (level, 5 mph)	7.0	7.7	8.4	9.1	9.8	10.5	11.1	11.8	12.5	13.2	13.9	14.6	15.2	15.9	16.6	17.3	18.0

Appendix C — Calorie Expenditure Per Minute for Various Activities (Continued) ....

Count only time of actual activity	BODY WEIGHT																
	90	99	108	117	125	134	143	152	161	170	178	187	196	205	213	222	231
Skiing (racing downhill)	9.9	10.9	11.9	12.9	13.7	14.7	15.7	16.7	17.7	18.7	19.6	20.6	21.6	22.6	23.4	24.4	25.4
Snowshoeing (2.3 mph)	3.7	4.1	4.5	4.8	5.2	5.5	5.9	6.3	6.7	7.0	7.4	7.8	8.1	8.5	8.8	9.2	9.6
Snowshoeing (2.5 mph)	5.4	5.9	6.5	7.0	7.5	8.0	8.6	9.1	9.7	10.2	10.7	11.2	11.8	12.3	12.8	13.3	13.9
Soccer	5.4	5.9	6.4	6.9	7.5	8.0	8.5	9.0	9.6	10.1	10.6	11.1	11.6	12.2	12.7	13.2	13.4
Squash	6.2	6.8	7.5	8.1	8.7	9.3	9.9	10.5	11.1	11.7	12.3	12.9	13.5	14.2	14.8	15.4	16.0
Swimming, pleasure 25 yds/min	3.6	4.0	4.3	4.7	5.0	5.4	5.7	6.1	6.4	6.8	7.1	7.5	7.8	8.2	8.5	8.9	9.2
Swimming, Back 20 yds/min	2.3	2.6	2.8	3.0	3.2	3.5	3.7	3.9	4.1	4.2	4.6	4.8	5.0	5.3	5.5	5.7	6.0
Swimming, Back 30 yds/min	3.2	3.5	3.8	4.1	4.4	4.7	5.1	5.4	5.7	6.0	6.3	6.6	6.9	7.2	7.4	7.9	8.2
Swimming, back 40 yds/min	5.0	5.5	5.8	6.5	7.0	7.5	7.9	8.5	8.9	9.4	9.9	10.4	10.9	11.4	11.9	12.3	12.8
Swimming, Breast 20 yds/min	2.9	3.2	3.4	3.8	4.0	4.3	4.6	4.9	5.1	5.4	5.7	6.0	6.3	6.5	6.8	7.1	7.4
Swimming, Breast 30 yds/min	4.3	4.8	5.2	5.7	6.0	6.4	6.9	7.3	7.7	8.1	8.6	9.0	9.4	9.9	10.3	10.8	11.1
Swimming, Breast 40 yds/min	5.8	6.3	6.9	7.5	8.0	8.6	9.2	9.7	10.3	10.8	11.4	12.0	12.5	13.1	13.7	14.2	14.8
Swimming, Butterfly 50 yds/min	7.0	7.7	8.4	9.1	9.8	10.5	11.1	11.9	12.5	13.2	13.9	14.6	15.2	15.9	16.6	17.3	18.0
Swimming, Crawl 20 yds/min	2.9	3.2	3.4	3.8	4.0	4.3	4.6	4.9	5.1	5.4	5.7	5.8	6.3	6.5	6.8	7.1	7.3
Swimming, Crawl 45 yds/min	5.2	5.8	6.3	6.8	7.3	7.8	8.3	8.8	9.3	9.8	10.4	10.9	11.4	11.9	12.4	12.9	13.4

Appendix C — Calorie Expenditure Per Minute for Various Activities (Continued) ....

Count only time of actual activity	BODY WEIGHT																
	90	99	108	117	125	134	143	152	161	170	178	187	196	205	213	222	231
Swimming, Crawl 50 yds/min	6.4	7.0	7.6	8.3	8.9	9.5	10.1	10.7	11.4	12.0	12.6	13.2	13.9	14.5	15.1	15.7	16.3
Table Tennis	2.3	2.6	2.8	3.0	3.2	3.5	3.7	3.9	4.1	4.2	4.6	4.8	5.0	5.3	5.5	5.7	6.0
Tennis (recreation)	4.2	4.6	5.0	5.4	5.8	6.2	6.6	7.0	7.4	7.8	8.2	8.6	9.0	9.4	9.8	10.2	10.6
Tennis (competition)	5.9	6.4	7.0	7.6	8.1	8.7	9.3	9.9	10.4	11.0	11.6	12.1	12.7	13.3	13.9	14.4	15.0
Timed Calisthenics	8.8	9.6	10.5	11.4	12.2	13.1	13.9	14.8	15.6	16.5	17.4	18.2	19.1	19.9	20.8	21.5	22.5
Volleyball (moderate)	3.4	3.8	4.0	4.4	4.8	5.1	5.4	5.8	6.1	6.4	6.8	7.1	7.4	7.8	8.1	8.3	8.8
Volleyball (vigorous)	5.9	6.4	7.0	7.6	8.1	8.7	9.3	9.9	10.4	11.0	11.6	12.1	12.7	13.3	13.9	14.4	15.0
Walking (2.0 mph)	2.1	2.3	2.5	2.7	2.9	3.1	3.3	3.5	3.7	4.0	4.2	4.4	4.6	4.8	5.0	5.2	5.4
Walking (4.5 mph)	4.0	4.4	4.7	5.1	5.5	5.9	6.3	6.7	7.1	7.5	7.8	8.2	8.6	9.0	9.4	9.8	10.1
Walking 110-120 steps/min	3.1	3.4	3.7	4.0	4.3	4.7	5.0	5.3	5.6	5.9	6.2	6.5	6.8	7.1	7.4	7.7	8.0
Waterskiing	4.7	5.1	5.6	6.1	6.5	7.0	7.4	7.9	8.3	8.8	9.3	9.7	10.2	10.6	11.1	11.5	12.0
Weight Training	4.7	5.1	5.7	6.2	6.7	7.0	7.5	7.9	8.4	8.9	9.4	9.9	10.3	10.8	11.1	11.7	12.2
XBX, Chart 1*	5.0	5.5	5.9	6.4	6.9	7.4	7.9	8.4	8.6	9.3	9.8	10.3	10.8	11.3	11.8	12.3	12.8
XBX, Chart 2*	6.2	6.9	7.5	8.1	8.7	9.3	9.9	10.5	11.1	11.7	12.3	12.9	13.6	14.2	14.8	15.4	16.0
XBX, Charts 3, 4*	8.8	9.6	10.5	11.4	12.2	13.1	13.9	14.8	15.6	16.5	17.4	18.2	19.1	19.9	20.8	21.6	22.5

*Canadian Ten Basic Exercise Programs.

Appendix D: Calories in common snack foods[1]

			Calories
1.	Apple (2½ inch diameter)	1	70
2.	Butter or margarine	1 pat	50
3.	Cake, chocolate, iced	1/16 of 10 inch diameter	445
4.	Cake, plain, chocolate icing	1/16 of 10 inch diameter	370
5.	Candy, caramels	1 oz.	115
6.	Candy, hard	1 oz.	110
7.	Candy, milk chocolate	1 oz.	150
8.	Cheese, Cheddar or American	1 inch cube	105
9.	Chili with beans, canned	1 cup	250
10.	Chocolate milk (skim milk)	1 cup	250
11.	Chocolate milkshake	12 oz. container	520
12.	Cocoa	1 cup	242
13.	Cookies, assorted (3 inch diameter)	1	120
*14.	Doughnuts, sugar	1	196
*15.	Frankfurter and roll	1	254
*16.	Hamburger	1½ oz., meat & roll, 1 tbs catsup	305
17.	Ice Cream	1 container, 4 fl. oz.	147
18.	Ice cream soda, chocolate	1 large glass	455
19.	Ice milk	½ cup, 4 fl. oz.	142
20.	Orange, navel (2 4/5 inch diameter)	1	60
21.	Pancakes (4 inch diameter)	1	60
22.	Peanuts, roasted, salted	¼ cup of halves	210

[1]Adapted from *Food and Your Weight*. Home and Garden Bulletin No. 74, U.S. Dept. of Agriculture. Washington, D. C.: U.S. Government Printing Office, revised edition, 1967.

*Counts for these items based on Bonomo, Joe. *Calorie Counter and Control Guide*. New York. Bonomo Calorie Books, Inc. (no date)

23. Pickles, large dill	1	15
24. Pie, apple	1/7 of 9 inch diameter	345
25. Pizza, cheese	5½ inch of 14 in. diameter	185
26. Popcorn, oil & salt	1 cup	65
27. Potatoes, French fried (2 x 1/2 x 1/2 inch)	10 pieces	155
28. Potato chips (2 inch diameter)	10 chips	115
29. Pretzels, small stick	5 sticks	20
30. Raisins	¼ cup	115
31. Syrup, table blends	1 tbs	60
32. Soft drinks		
cola type	10 oz.	118
ginger ale	10 oz.	87
33. Spaghetti with meatballs	1 cup	335
34. Sugar	1 tsp	15
35. Waffles, 1/2 x 4½ x 5½ inches	1	210
36. Yogurt; partially skim milk	1 cup	120

Appendix E: Questions and answers

MULTIPLE CHOICE

1. All body movement is characterized by
   a. direction, force, and speed   d. all of these
   b. level, color, and tone   e. none of these
   c. locomotor and propulsive qualities
2. The force which makes movement possible is supplied by contraction of
   a. ligaments   b. fascia   c. muscles   d. tendons   (p. 5)
3. Maintaining the body in an erect position is mostly a question of opposing
   a. gravity   b. leverage   c. force   d. buoyancy   (p. 9)
4. Body type is
   a. of no importance in determining appearance
   b. changes at intervals throughout life
   c. is inherited
   d. depends upon the quantity of food eaten.   (p. 4)
5. In a well-balanced standing position the pull of gravity
   a. is decreased   c. is ahead of the base
   b. is increased   d. is equally distributed   (p. 9)
6. The attainment of well-balanced standing posture is important because
   a. we stand still more than we sit or move about
   b. the ideal posture is the least fatiguing
   c. the vital organs are impaired by poor standing habits
   d. good standing posture is aesthetically pleasing   (pp. 48-49)
7. Poor standing posture is largely a result of
   a. weak musculature   c. careless habits
   b. carrying heavy books to school   d. fatigue   (p. 51)
8. Body balance when standing is improved by
   a. standing on the balls of the feet
   b. reaching the arms overhead
   c. thrusting the shoulders back and the hips forward
   d. all of these
   e. none of these   (pp. 49-50)

9. Standing with feet apart instead of together
   a. lowers the center of gravity
   b. raises the center of gravity
   c. displaces the center of gravity to one side
   d. has no effect on the center of gravity   (p. 11)

10. When walking rapidly, the normal movement pattern should be changed by
    a. increasing lateral motion   c. increasing the knee bend
    b. leaning backward from the ankles   d. eliminating arm swing   (p. 57)

11. In walking, the movement to step forward should be initiated at the
    a. waist   b. hips   c. knee   d. ankle   e. toes   (p. 56)

12. In running rapidly
    a. the heel should strike the ground first
    b. the lower leg should swing well up and back
    c. the arms should swing diagonally toward the mid-body line
    d. all of these
    e. none of these   (p. 59)

13. In landing from a jump one should
    a. flex the knees   d. all of these
    b. flex the ankles   e. none of these   (p. 17)
    c. flex the hips

14. The principle "apply force through the center of gravity" is illustrated in
    a. slicing a golf ball   c. extending the legs to rise from a squat
    b. delivering a bowling ball d. leaning across a table to raise a window

15. If the knees remain straight while picking up a typewriter from the floor, the main
    work is done by the
    a. hands and fingers   c. thighs
    b. back   d. calves   (pp. 15, 26-27)

16. In pulling a heavy object toward you, the feet should be
    a. separated forward and back   d. turned to toe out
    b. separated sideward   e. turned to toe in
    c. together   (pp. 12, 15)

17. The body should be kept erect when
    a. climbing stairs   c. pushing   e. none of these
    b. running   d. all of these   (pp. 15, 58, 59)

18. In pushing against a wall, the working muscles are in a state of
    a. static contraction   c. independent relaxation
    b. eccentric contraction   d. isotonic stretch   (p. 6)

19. The most graceful of these sitting positions is
    a. hips well forward on the chair seat
    b. legs crossed at the knee
    c. feet parallel and squarely placed on the floor
    d. ankles crossed   (pp. 53-54)

20. The most efficient way to carry a heavy bag of groceries is
    a. to thrust the hips sideways to support the weight
    b. to lean slightly backward from the ankles
    c. to lock the knees firmly
    d. to walk with the feet separated laterally   (pp. 11-12)

21. One should *not* undertake a strenuous conditioning program
    a. after the age of 30
    b. if engaged in a sedentary occupation
    c. if engaged in work involving emotional tension
    d. without a preliminary medical examination
    e. if overweight   (p. 42)

22. The primary conditioning effect of rope jumping is to develop
    a. arm and leg strength
    b. abdominal strength
    c. shoulder flexibility
    d. coordination
    e. circulorespiratory endurance
    (p. 43)

23. To develop endurance it is necessary to
    a. overexert   b. overlearn   c. overload   d. overdo   e. overwork

24. Strength can best be developed by
    a. progressive resistance exercise
    b. gradually increasing the number of repetitions of an exercise
    c. running a mile every day
    d. free-swinging, relaxed, and rhythmic movements
    (p. 19)

25. Strength may be developed by
    a. isotonic exercise
    b. isometric exercise
    c. isokinetic exercise
    d. all of these
    (p. 19)

26. Kinesthetic perception is essential in learning
    a. to stand correctly
    b. to play tennis
    c. to relax consciously
    d. all of these
    e. none of these

27. The best of these activities for developing all-around flexibility is
    a. archery
    b. basketball
    c. folk dance
    d. modern dance
    e. softball

28. A batter uses a back swing
    a. to develop speed
    b. to hit the ball squarely
    c. because the bat is heavy
    d. so he can "give" on contact with the ball
    (p. 16)

29. Muscle soreness after exercise is best relieved by
    a. a cold shower
    b. moderate exercise
    c. alternate hot and cold packs
    d. complete rest
    e. all-out exercise
    (p. 27)

30. The muscles most strengthened by stair climbing and descending are on the
    a. backs of the thighs
    b. fronts of the thighs
    c. abdomen
    d. lower back
    e. soles of the feet

31. By practicing an exercise in which you jump to place feet apart and clap hands over head and then return to position, the normal college student could expect to improve
    a. shoulder flexibility
    b. leg flexibility
    c. hip flexibility
    d. none of these
    e. all of these
    (pp. 25-27)

32. Among the muscles strengthened by the push-up exercise are the
    a. abdominals, pectorals, and muscles on outsides of arms
    b. pectorals, backs of thighs, and lower back muscles
    c. abdominals, calf, and inner arm muscles
    d. lower back, and fronts of leg muscles and gluteals
    (p. 75)

33. Clasping the hands in front of the chest and then pulling as if to separate the hands is a form of exercise known as
    a. isometric
    b. force versus force
    c. equal effort
    d. concentric
    e. isotonic
    (p. 19)

34. Picking up small objects with the toes is a good exercise
    a. to make the ankles flexible
    b. to strengthen the longitudinal arch
    c. to stretch the heel cord
    d. to increase pronation
    (p. 76)

35. The reason for contracting muscle groups while practicing relaxation is
    a. to learn to contrast the feel of tension and relaxation
    b. to fatigue the muscles so that they are ready to relax

    c. to develop strength in all body parts
    d. to keep the mind occupied   (p. 67)

36. The ability to relax consciously is important in
    a. sports   c. gymnastics   e. none of these
    b. dance   d. all of these

37. Backaches frequently are caused by
    a. sitting in straight chairs   d. vertebrae out of line
    b. overdeveloped back muscles   e. weak abdominal muscles
    c. eyestrain   (p. 65)

38. Caloric requirement depends upon
    a. metabolic rate   d. all of these
    b. work performed   e. none of these
    c. temperature in which work is done   (p. 35)

39. The best weight reducing diet includes
    a. protein only   c. all food types   e. little liquid or salt
    b. no carbohydrates   d. liquids only   (p. 34)

40. Dieting for weight reduction cannot be considered to have been successful until
    a. five pounds have been lost   d. desirable new eating habits have been
    b. ten pounds have been lost   established
    c. spot reduction has occurred   e. the hips are three inches smaller
                                         (pp. 33-35)

TRUE OR FALSE

T F 41. A muscle must expend energy in order to lengthen.   (p. 5)

T F 42. If during contraction a muscle shortens, it is performing isometric exercise.
                                                       (p. 19)

T F 43. In order to maintain equilibrium it is necessary for the center of gravity to be centered above the base.   (p. 9)

T F 44. For stability, the knee joints should be braced backward.   (p. 49)

T F 45. In isotonic exercise muscles contract forcefully but do not move the body parts.   (p. 19)

T F 46. A normal heart cannot be injured by strenuous exercise.

T F 47. It takes considerable energy and time to maintain a state of good condition.
                                                       (p. 21)

T F 48. Every college woman should devote 30 minutes a day to conditioning regardless of her specific purposes.

T F 49. Once acquired, a state of fitness can be retained with little or no further exercise.   (p. 31)

T F 50. The most intense exercise in a work-out period should be performed at the middle of the session.   (p. 31)

T F 51. As long as the same amount of time is spent on a conditioning program each month, the spacing, duration, and regularity of the exercise is unimportant.
                                                       (p. 31)

T F 52. A well-conditioned individual breathes more slowly than the untrained.

T F 53. Mobility of the hand and foot are comparable.

T F 54. Abdominal exercise facilitates the return of venous blood to the heart. (p. 61)

T F 55. Sports and dance have no legitimate place in a conditioning program. (p. 43)

T F 56. Fatigue is a necessary part of building endurance.   (pp. 22-23)

T F 57. A college woman with excellent muscle tone and endurance should be able to do 50 sit-ups.

T   F   58. Breathing should be continuous when moving heavy objects.

T   F   59. The leg rather than the back muscles should be used for heavy lifting. (p. 27)

T   F   60. Toe touching is a good exercise for the abdominal muscles.   (pp. 26-27)

T   F   61. Good posture is the most efficient body alignment for a given task.

T   F   62. The key to good standing posture is the position of the pelvis.

T   F   63. The "ideal" standing posture is a model to which everyone should conform
        exactly.   (p. 50)

T   F   64. Right handed people tend to hold the right shoulder lower than the left.

T   F   65. Since standing posture is highly individualized, it does not matter how one
        stands.   (p. 48)

T   F   66. If the force of gravity is unopposed, standing posture will be good.   (p. 9)

T   F   67. A correctly tilted pelvis is unlikely in the presence of forward shoulders. (p. 51)

T   F   68. There is a considerable amount of shoulder movement in a graceful walk.
                                                                             (p. 57)

T   F   69. In running, it is desirable to use a smaller base of support than in walking.
                                                                             (p. 59)

T   F   70. The most important point to remember for the sake of appearance in entering
        and leaving an automobile is to keep the hips low.   (p. 54)

T   F   71. Toeing out is a graceful foot position in descending stairs.   (p. 58)

T   F   72. It is more conspicuous to turn to face a door as you shut it than to close
        the door behind your back.   (p. 55)

T   F   73. Toe curling is a good exercise for the metatarsal arch.   (p. 64)

T   F   74. Dysmenorrhea is more often the result of functional than of structural causes.
                                                                             (p. 61)

T   F   75. The energy expended by a tense person is useful because the resulting fatigue
        induces sleep.   (p. 66)

T   F   76. Preliminary to the take-off in a jump for distance it is important to decrease
        body stability.   (p. 16)

T   F   77. Throwing and catching require isotonic muscular contraction.   (p. 19)

T   F   78. The backswing which precedes a throw or a hit adds force to it.

T   F   79. "Giving" when one catches a ball absorbs some of its force.   (p. 17)

T   F   80. A weight loss of five pounds per week when dieting is a reasonable expectation
        for most college women.   (p. 35)

T   F   81. In a program to lose weight it is more important to do twisting and kneading
        exercises than endurance exercises.   (pp. 34, 37)

T   F   82. The best body weight is the average weight for age, sex, and height. (p. 87)

T   F   83. Calories come from both carbohydrate and fat consumption.   (p. 36)

T   F   84. Electrical stimulation of muscle fibers has proved an effective means of spot
        reducing.

T   F   85. Exercise should be avoided when trying to gain weight.   ˙   (p. 36)

COMPLETION

86. The balance point of the body of an object is called the _____ .   (p. 9)

87. A phenomenon during strenuous exercise in which the "out of breath" feeling sud-
    denly diminishes is called _____ .   (p. 22)

88. As the degree of fitness increases, the heart rate tends to _____ and the blood
    output per stroke tends to _____ .   (p. 21)

89. Even resting muscles are in a slightly contracted state known as _____ .   (p. 5)

90. Muscles that contract to oppose a movement are known as the _____.   (p. 6)
91. Anatomical differences favor the _____ sex in body stability.   (p. 59)
92. The work load of a conditioning exercise can be made heavier by increasing the _____, the _____, and the _____.   (p. 28)
93. By means of the _____ sense, we are aware of the location of the parts of the body in relation to one another.   (p. 51)
94. Exercises requiring a full squat position are frowned on by some experts for fear of injury to the _____.   (p. 28)
95. When rotary motion is the desired outcome, force should be applied at the _____ of an object.   (p. 16)
96. Flattening the arc of the delivery makes for greater _____ in throwing.
97. Transference of the body weight forward in throwing or striking is for the purpose of _____.   (p. 16)
98. The posture fault in which the weight is carried over the inner borders of the feet is called _____ .   (p. 63)
99. The _____ exercise is for prevention of functional dysmenorrhea.   (p. 62)
100. At the end of a vigorous period of exercise, appetite tends to _____ .   (p. 34)

ANSWERS TO EVALUATION QUESTIONS

*No answer

Page	Answer and Page Reference
10	1. *
	2. No (p. 9)
	3. Center of gravity must be over the base of support for equilibrium. (p. 9)
11	Center of gravity must be over the base of support for equilibrium and stability is greater when the center of gravity is low. (pp. 9, 11)
12	*
	It would be awkward to walk bent over in order to lower the center of gravity. (pp. 11-12)
13	Yes. The position in which more of the body is in contact with the floor because the center of gravity is lower. (pp. 9, 11)
26	*
	Trunk flexibility (pp. 25-26)
29	*
36	*
44	*
50	*, *
53	*
65	With feet apart and parallel, bend knees and grasp bar with thumbs under. Start lifting bar by extending knees forcefully. Then step forward under bar bringing it to the top of the chest with elbows under bar and forearms vertical. (pp. 15, 65)

ANSWERS TO TEST QUESTIONS

Multiple Choice

1. A	10. C	19. D	28. A	37. E
2. C	11. B	20. B	29. B	38. D
3. A	12. E	21. D	30. B	39. C
4. C	13. D	22. E	31. D	40. D
5. D	14. C	23. C	32. A	
6. D	15. B	24. A	33. A	
7. C	16. A	25. C	34. B	
8. E	17. A	26. D	35. A	
9. A	18. A	27. D	36. D	

True or False

41. F	50. T	59. T	68. F	77. T
42. F	51. F	60. F	69. T	78. T
43. T	52. T	61. T	70. T	79. T
44. F	53. F	62. T	71. F	80. F
45. T	54. T	63. F	72. T	81. F
46. T	55. F	64. T	73. F	82. F
47. F	56. T	65. F	74. T	83. T
48. F	57. T	66. F	75. F	84. F
49. F	58. T	67. T	76. T	85. F

Completion

86. center of gravity	92. speed, resistance, number of repetitions	96. accuracy
87. second wind		97. increasing distance
88. decrease, increase	93. kinesthetic	98. pronation
89. tonus	94. knee	99. Billig
90. antagonists	95. edge	100. decrease
91. female		

Index